MY ROAD

From A Trail – To A Super Highway

"ONLY IN AMERICA"

By CHARLES E. WILLIAMS

© 2011 Charles E. Williams. All Rights Reserved.

All rights reserved under International and Pan-African Copyright Conventions. No part of this publication may be reproduced or transmitted in any form or by any means, electronic or mechanical, including photocopy, recording, or information storage and retrieval system, without the written permission of the Author.

Published in the United States of America by
Publishing Associates, Inc., Atlanta, Georgia.
ISBN: 978-0-942683-06-6
A library quality casebound book.
For book orders, author appearance inquiries and interviews, contact the Publisher by mail at:

Publishing Associates, Inc.
5020 Montcalm Drive
Atlanta, Georgia 30331
Fcpublish@aol.com.
Cover photo credit: Eric Fitchpatric
Book Design: RM Productions

Library of Congress Cataloging In Publication Data

MY ROAD

From A Trail – To A Super Highway
"ONLY IN AMERICA"

By Charles E. Williams

Publishing Associates, Inc.
Atlanta, Georgia

My Road

A journey that started on trail in west central Alabama over seven decades ago…

My road, as I call it began as a mission of promise supported by persons of little means but of great principle and dignity during a period in our country's history that was very difficult and puzzling for many of us. There was no reliable yardstick by which one could accurately predict a future. The humble little path that I started out on was not very well defined; it was laced with many irritating obstacles and was not in very good condition. It led me to a small road that was loaded with curves, hills, valleys, ditches, small creeks and eventually to the hard surface highway. After reaching the hard surface road, I was rewarded by a feeling that this path would one day take me to the super highway and the fast lanes. This unusual connectivity of road network could only happen in America, where one could start at the bottom and through hard work, courage and much prayer, end up on the top. So, this is a life story that must be told … and now! The timing of this story is significant because it represents a venue to honored institutions and acumen that will allow them to proclaim their place as professionals, business owners and community leaders. Many young people today are trying to find a path from their current state of being to a meaningful future. My road is proof that you can get there.

Table of Contents

Dedication .... v.
Acknowledgements... vii.
Preface .... xiii.
Introduction xv
Chapter 1 – Early Life... 17
    Mother's Passing.. 21
    Grandmother's Role 22
    Family & Etc.. 24
Chapter 2 – Career Preparation 27
    Elementary School Experience 27
    The School 28
    Junior and High School Experience................................... 29
    University/College Experience 30
    Finding My Wife... 39
Chapter 3 – Starting the Career.. 43
    Army Officer (Engineer).. 43
    Our First Car 44
    Operation Swift Strike... 47
    Flight School & Germany Assignment 49
Chapter 4 – Vietnam War 57
    Experience... 57
    My Impression 64
Chapter 5 – Starting the Climb 69
    Graduate School.. 69
    Development of Management Style................................... 71
    Military Schooling – Mid Level... 72
    First Washington Assignment.. 73
    Battalion Command Assignment....................................... 76
Chapter 6 – Entering into the Fast Lane................................... 79
    Army War College... 79
    Brigade Command Experience 82
    Re-building the Tank Ranges... 84
    The Range Modernization Project 85
    German/American Relations 96

  Command of Brigade 98
  Selection to Brigadier General 102
  Patty at University of Virginia (UVA) 104
  Chuck, Jr. at West Point (USMA).................................... 104
  Calvin at Virginia Military Institute (VMI) 105
  My Wife's Reflections On "My Road" 106

Photo Section 109

Chapter 7 – The Big Hills 147
  Director of Operations and Maintenance 149
  North Atlantic Division Commander............................. 152
  Regional VP of Society American Military Engineers 154
  Re-building of Ft. Drum 157
  Moving toward the Results-Based Organization Concept 160
  Back to Washington – Pentagon, Director of Mgmt 162

Chapter 8 – Helping the Children... 167
  New York City School Construction Authority 167
  Paradigm Shift – How we did it 177

Chapter 9 - First Private Toll Road in VA in 150 years................ 185
  Why the Fast Track... 186
  Helping the Children Again 204

Chapter 10 – The Crown Jewel 207
  Great Leader (Gen. Colin L. Powell) – Secretary of State. 208

Chapter 11 - Interview of OBO Director 213
  Results Based Operations (RBO) Concept 234
  The Results – Building New Embassies/Consulates 237
  A New Management Approach 239
  The Transformation 242
  My Visit to Iraq (Baghdad)... 246
  The Bottom Line 248
  A Concluding Note 249
  State of Alabama – The Roots... 251
  Charles E. Williams.. 252

Index 255

Dedication

This book is dedicated to my great grandmother, Annie Long Ellis, affectionately known to us as "Bannie," who was blessed to live long enough to see our country from so many different vantage points. She was truly one of those sages and mentors who have been the backbone of the African American family and community. Bannie did so much to set me and my siblings on the right path and direction in life. She was a truly remarkable human being. This strong, but humble and wonderful lady was there when I was born; was there when I went off to school for the first time; was there when it was time to go to church; was there when I drove a car for the first time; was there when my mother died, and yes was there when I went off to college and when I got married. Her quiet but strong voice echoes today and will always be remembered as the "tone setter" for my life's path. So, the dedication of this publication of "My Road" is my way of saying to her, "I listened to you, heard what you said and tried very hard to make you proud." So, continue to rest in peace.

Acknowledgements

I could never have written this book without the support, understanding, encouragement and love of my wife, Marjorie and our three children, Patty, Chuck Jr., and Calvin. My dear wife who has been on this journey with me over fifty years, and has put up with many long days of writing and sometimes even grouchy days to get this done. She deserves all the thanks I can offer for her patience and understanding.

I also wish to offer special thanks to the publisher, Fred Cleveland and Publishing Associates, Inc. of Atlanta, GA., who took this task on and got it done for me. The meticulous documentation and producing the first rough drafts of my writings for this book all was done entirely by Song Keller. She spent countless hours with intense research and many double checks to get the rough manuscript ready for a final review. An amazing performance by a devoted assistant who deserves my thanks.

*The power and ability to rise above your circumstances
and achieve the results you desire resides within you.*

— *Roger Connors*

Preface

My Road is a unique account of one American's life story who gave so much and asked for so little from his country. A career that took shape by serving 29 years in the Army as a pilot and a Corps of Engineers officer, eight years in the private sector as a senior executive, and another seven years again in the government at the appointed senior executive level. He managed the modernization of new tank ranges and associated facilities in Germany; the rebuilding of Ft. Drum, a major Army installation upstate New York; building of new and renovating schools in New York City; the design and building of the first private Toll Road in Virginia in 150 years, and the design and building of over 50 US Embassy/Consulate compounds around the world. This steely, smart and well mannered man traveled and worked in every region of the world and saw people in the worse and best situations. It was truly "his road."

He carved out his space carefully, kept his mind sharp and maintained a very clear focus through continuous study, watched over and provided for his family, stayed connected to his church and traveled "his road" and made it to the super highway. His road is truly another American story that is deeply rooted in what makes this country great. In this book, it will become clear why this man has been called another Moses, the master builder, a Captain of his Industry, one of the rare breed selected for his state's Hall of Fame in Engineering and Construction, an Engineering News Record Markman, an Engineering News Record Newsmaker, Chairman of the Board of Trustees of Tuskegee University, a General, a father, grandfather and a devoted husband.

My Road: From A Trail – To A Super Highway captures the life and experience of Charles E. Williams, a man who started from a very humble and modest beginning and chose a path through life that landed him at a place that was as good as it could get. Since this "road" was not easy and it required the best every day, it is unique and interesting to follow and learn how it took shape through the years. This could only happen in the United States of America for this Man. His story brings into focus the "road" that was taken to move from a small trail to a super highway. The amazing aspect about this treatment of "My Road" is how skillfully the author laced certain central themes that clearly define this road and the many "sign posts" and people who helped him serve the greater good with wisdom, leadership and by example.

Williams' inspiring words underpin what this life path is all about. He says, "There was no choice for me but to learn early in my life how the system works and get up on my feet and go out and find my own path and began this journey.

In spite of all that has been written and said about our country, "My Road" could only have happened in America. It is true that there were obstacles and a few elements of unfairness along the way, but it was still enough space for me to get up, work hard and learn how the system works and go out and travel my path. It was simply beyond my biggest dream to know that my career journey would end up at the place it did. For that, I am deeply grateful and thankful for the opportunity to write this story. "My Road" is sprinkled with a few opportunities, some half crack doors, several disappointments and my best recollection of how this "road" was knitted together over 70+ years."

Introduction
Life is a Cafeteria

One day a grandfather told his grand children about his family's ordeal of getting to America. He told of the ships and all that to the family members from their home in Africa. He recounted how they had been hurdle once they arrived in this country and how afterward some survived, and he being a descendent had gone to a cafeteria in Lower Manhattan to get something to eat.

He sat down at an empty table and waited for someone to come and take his order. After a while when no one came, a woman with a full tray of food sat down opposite of him and explained how the cafeteria works. "You start at that end", she said, pointing toward a stack of trays, "then go along the food line and pick out what you want. At the other end, they will tell you how much you must pay."

The grandfather reflected a moment and then told his grandchildren, "I soon learned that's how everything works in America." Life is a cafeteria here. You can get anything you want, even very great success if you are willing to pay the price. But you will never get what you want if you waited for someone to bring it to you. You have to get up and get it yourself.

So from this forward – get up and get your life organized now.

—*Author Unknown*

One

Early Life

Time is too slow for those who wait, too swift for those who fear, too long for those who grieve, too short for those who rejoice, but for those who love, time is eternity. Hours fly, flowers die, new days, new ways, pass by. Love stays. —Henry Van Dyke

I believe this author has it right. We are all different and our starting point in the big race of life is not at the same place. I learned early that we all have our own race to run and each of us will discover our own pathways. As a result, I never looked back very much. The present and going forward was what gave me encouragement and strength to press ahead. This was the reality that I experienced along "My Road."

Sawyerville, Alabama is located in the central part of the state between Tusculoosa and Greensboro, in Hale county. This region was called the "Black Belt," because of its rich natural resources, some of the best for farming and forest areas in the country. It was heavily populated with black farm workers, laborers, and craftsmen who lived in primarily segregated communities.

My Dad, Roosevelt Williams, was a farmer and timber cutter. He specialized in pulpwood harvesting, cutting pulp or cord wood from small trees. He also sometimes trimmed the tops of trees that were cut for logs. My Dad had a unique talent for clearing land and gained the respect of many people in the area for his ability to transfer woods into useful land for farming. He also had relationships with sawmills that purchased timber.

The glimmer of hope for the black inhabitants were the successful and newsworthy people they celebrated who had achieved notoriety as graduates from nearby historically black colleges and universities (HBCU's) such as Alabama A&M, Miles College, Taladega, Alabama State, Stillman, Clark College, Spelman and Morehouse in Atlanta not to mention the renowned Tuskegee Institute. Tuskegee in particular was known to produce many of the areas teachers, nurses, and other professionals. Booker T. Washington, its founder was one the most influential black person of his time. Scientist and educator George Washington Carver's discoveries in agriculture revived farming in the South. The Tuskegee Airmen were renowned for their contribution to World War II with their flying missions, and unique accomplishments as military professionals. As one of America's most honored institutions, Tuskegee University has the distinction of having many firsts among their graduates; African American generals and other officers, scientists, professors, nurses and theologians. Black America gravitated to the armed forces and to Tuskegee and other HBCU's because of the proud example demonstrated by its students. As a result, throughout my young life, the people who impressed me most were ministers, teachers, doctors, and others who were graduates of these institutions. It stood to reason that I would desire to be among those who would attend such a marvelous center of learning that would prepare me to come back to my community with my talents as did many of the people I most admired.

Our community was a rural farming area of working class blacks and whites who mostly owned their land and worked as farmers and laborers. Because of my father's unique talent of clearing forests, he became a valuable and respected resource to our neighbors and those who hired him. As the son of a preacher and a second generation resident he was considered a merchant of sorts that earned the respect of those in the community beyond the barriers of race. He had a team of workers comprised of my older brother, a cousin, and a couple of others who were known as "Cootes boys." I worked with him as his record keeper and in later years as his truck driver. I assisted him in keeping his ledger updated of the terms projects, man hours, costs and payments. Back then, a ledger was like a bible or an official record that would hold up in court if there were any disputes. Customers would call my dad to clear woods for thinning or they desired to have as additional farm land or for new buildings. He could estimate a fair cost to clear the land as well as determine what a track of forest would bring at the sawmill and even the quantity it would bring as ground pulp.

My dad drove an old ford truck with a flat bed for the pulpwood work. He kept a Bible opened on his dashboard always, right next to his ledger. This is before the days of *USA Today* so as a young avid reader, I read his Bible quite frequently between the ledger entries. I would marvel as to how his concepts and promises came together.

His work ethic was meticulous and grueling. His word was his bond. He saw to it that the lessons of integrity were evident in everyone he served. He was medium in stature, but certainly pound for pound the strongest man I'd ever seen for a person of his size. I once saw him pick up the rear of a car that was stuck in the mud. He was also handy as a self-made brick mason, pouring cement and building extensions to our home, smokehouse or garages. He always rendered a lesson to me or any of my brothers who assisted him in these projects. He was quite a renaissance man.

My mother, Mattie Wallace Williams was from Akron, Alabama, a small town about five miles from Sawyerville. She and my Dad grew up together in the same area. Their families knew each other well. Mother came from a large family. She was a beautiful, soft spoken woman who was small in stature with a purposeful and commanding presence in a crowded home. She was humble and had the gift of making each of us feel as if we were her greatest concern. We were like stair steps without an ending; 7 boys and 2 girls. There was Roosevelt Jr., Luther, Willie, Robert, Emma, Arthur, James, Rubye and me. The members of the household and mother worked together perfectly. She was never at a loss for endearing comments or attention to each of her children. She managed to keep everyone fed and our house in order. She taught my sisters about canning, food preparation, budgeting, cooking and housekeeping. She ran a tight ship and always knew the right thing to say. Most of mother's siblings followed each other north to Detroit and Chicago where jobs in automobile plants and factories were plentiful and housing and northern schools were available. The aunt who we became more familiar with was Aunt Laura, who lived in the same general area.

Every Sunday we journeyed the two mile trip to the church as a family including Bannie, our great-grandmother, who was the mother of the church and one of the oldest persons in our community. Everyone respected our parent's rule that we attend church on Sunday. Following church we had Sunday dinner with many of the delectables the women had prepared. Church was the gathering place where we met neighbors, classmates and friends and caught up with area news. It was a great venue for communication in those days.

Mother's Passing

A very dramatic and troubling event occurred early in my life on February 28, 1953 – my mother died at age 37-1/2.

I was old enough to understand and comprehend it all and hearing my mother saying to me as I left for school that late winter day, "study hard today, do well in school and do not worry because everything with me will be alright." So it was - family members met the school bus that afternoon to inform my brother and me that our mother (mama) had passed away. At age 14-1/2, this was a terrific blow that left me numb for a very long time and bothers me even today, I cannot completely reconcile the "why." I remember that she had delivered a still born baby, and had been in the hospital as a result and was back home and was very sick. From that very confusing afternoon, I realized clearly that life is loaded with both joy and pain, and my "road" from this day forward was not going to be easy to navigate. My mother was full of energy and was always busy trying to help someone else. For her, giving wasn't something that she did, it was who she was and her way of life. I decided to stay with the same path that was started while my mother was living (finishing school and working towards professional career). The picture of my life's pathway was so clear that afternoon and with exception of few blurs along the way, it remains clear as I traveled my road. It was a simple picture that requires one to work through one issue or event at a time while still maintaining a focus on where you wanted to go. As I grew in age and experience, I was never able to really come to grip with the reason why this had to happen to me so early in my life. I learned to condition myself to live with it and use the event as a building block for character going forward. A mother's passing does not end our relationship with her -- for her identity has become our own, our life her greatest gift.

This was my first bump into reality where I had to make an assessment of the current state and look across that rough terrain to a desired state. I knew there was much hard work ahead.

Grandmother's Role

Life is a masterpiece but you must be the one who allows the brush to touch the canvas. —Tony Sinclair

Annie Long Ellis, affectionately known to all as "Bannie," was my great grandmother, a marvelous spirit who stepped out of full retirement to assume the role of caretaker for our family at the untimely passing of our mother. There were nine of us; shocked and broken by loss of our mother, but it was Bannie who exhibited a richness in faith and embraced us all with her strong belief in the power of the Almighty. She comforted us through our loss and helped us take charge of his or her own destiny.

My great grandmother lived next door and on the day after mother's death, she came in and took control of the domestic side of the family activities. She gave tough love and orders to each of us, (my father included) and anyone else who was in her sight. She knew how to prepare large quantity food servings and always insured that we had plenty to eat and our clothes were clean, manners were correct and our homework was done every night. The amazing quality of how she handled adversity was remarkable. It takes love for another to lay your life, your schedule, and your own needs down for another. According to Galatians it is the greatest form of love. That is what Bannie demonstrated to us. She also had a keen sense of how the social issues in the country at that time were unfolding. She often talked about how the terrible issue of slavery bent the thinking of so many people and pointed out then that it was going to take many years for those wounds to heal. I knew then that this storm was going to be around for a while. She was somewhat of a subject matter expert since she was only a generation or two removed from the ordeal.

In the face of racism, both blatant and subtle, financial struggles, and personal setbacks, black grandmothers have helped their families in thousands of tangible and intangible ways, providing support, inspiration, and love not only to their own children and grandchildren but also to neighbors, friends, and extended families.

In those days, I was as full of questions as Bannie was of answers. A pillar of strength, here stood a woman who could've easily been overwhelmed with the responsibilities of living, caring for her great grandchildren, and just plain keeping her head above water. Whoever said no one is irreplaceable never met my great-grandmother. Though she is no longer with us, but her advice continues to make a difference in unexpected and unexplained ways.

The toughness in holding her position and the calm compassion in dealing with us when things were not going in the right direction were outstanding traits. I was so impressed that my thinking was truly shaped by this wonderful person who never allowed me or any of my sisters and brothers to see her cry. When things were bothering her, and even in happy times she would hum one of her favorite Negro hymns. I can remember so well hearing her humming, *Jesus keep me near the cross.*

I learned that life would be loaded with some joy and some pain; every person had to find a way to carry his/her load; it did not make sense to join a fight that was not yours, and to always do your big thinking about tomorrow. Bannie, my great grandmother, was truly an amazing lady who played a pivotal role in shaping my critical thinking about the world, our country and our people.

She lived for 114 years and had a mind crisp enough at 110 years old to recite to me the names and birthdays of my three children. A phenomenal woman to say the least!

Family & Etc.

My entire family elders were fortunate to own land and their modest homes. They worked very hard and made a decent living. They were able to provide us with the basics and much love. Since my family owned connecting land, this allowed my grandfather and father the opportunity to do some farming as well as to have a regular job. We raised green vegetables, some fruits and shared them among the family and neighbors who had something to share. My grandfather was a Methodist minister and spent much of his time handling the work associated with his church.

My Dad, Roosevelt Williams, was a man of great faith also. He was the strongest and hardest working person I have ever known. He farmed and managed his own small pulp wood harvesting business. He was an engineer of sorts, one who could lay out and direct the clearing of a wooded site, using heavy equipment to clear areas for building or farming.

He also dabbled in construction around the home. My dad was a jack of all trades and it was by working with him, I became curious at a very young age about the notion of how brick, mortar and lumber could be used to build buildings that would not fall down.

My father was very active in our church and was a good man who loved his children. It was the family rule – we had no choice other than to attend and participate in church activities every Sunday. It was really fun as we grew up to do this. My brothers and sisters: Roosevelt, Luther, Willie, Robert, Emma, Arthur, James and Rubye; were all decent students as five of us finished college —three with PhD degrees, one with a master's degree and one with a B.S. degree— and all own their homes and have successful careers. We credit so much of this accomplishment to the strong and kind touch by our great grandmother and the hard work ethic of our father.

While we live today in different places, the memories and love are so present in each of us. Our family has always been very close and really enjoys being together especially on special occasions. The one occasion that is most appreciated is the July 4th holiday barbecue that takes place back at the home place in Alabama. We reminisce about how all this got started, laugh, joke and sometimes shed a few tears of joy. As we advance in age, we consider each year's meeting a true blessing and resolve ourselves to be about full disclosure regarding each other's health. Its become somewhat of an annual check-up. We lost our brother Arthur, in 2010, which makes us all conscious of how fortunate we have been to have lived such a rewarding life with so many wonderful offspring. It is always a delight to revisit our birth place and reflect on the family. We all agree that we come away feeling refreshed that "only in America" could a story like this unfold as it did.

We had our share of disappointments and unexpected or hurtful experiences growing up as a family. A close family bond enabled us to weather uncertainties and the occasional accident or mishap that would occur among high energy young people living in a small space. Those experiences proved to make us stronger as we reflect today. Among the nine of us; we all had some type of hard fall growing up. The three toughest for us was a gunshot wound that occurred while two of my brothers were playing with a shot gun. There was also a rather serious automobile accident involving one of my brothers, and as you will learn later, there was my own accident while in college.

Those were accidents that were a part of just "getting through it." We were all thankful that none of those situations caused anyone to loose their life. These events were great sign posts for me as I traveled my road.

Two

Early Preparation

The future belongs to those who believe in the beauty of their dreams. —*Eleanor Roosevelt*

Elementary School Experience

My elementary school education was very unique in that I started to school two years prior to the age of six. Since we walked to school (about 1-1/2 miles) and my older brother was not comfortable going to school alone, my parents sent me along to school with him. It was not their intent for me to formally attend school then but it just happened. I naturally gravitated to learning and the teachers welcomed my enthusiasm to learn. I was blessed to be a fast learner and in fact, I beat out most of the regular students, just out of sheer desire. There was no early education or kindergarten available to me as four year old. The rules in those days were somewhat accommodating for a young student who was considered a "smart" kid so I was allowed to start school officially two years early. I was a very small young fellow and always stayed clear of any fights or big tussles on the playground or while en route to and from school. My teachers were kind and really encouraged me academically to be the best I could be. I was game for the challenge. Within a short while I became one of the best at spelling and math. I would always set on the front seat so the teacher could see me (and yes, protect me) during classes. In those days, there were some rather seasoned six graders in that same class with size to match.

The School

Flatwood Elementary was a school within a church building, an important staple in Alabama's indigenous history and culture. It was an old building of wood structure with no indoor plumbing and a list of repairs that needed attention. The school yard and the unpaved lot were the only areas available for recreation and outside activities. Heating came from a coal/wood heater that was situated in the center of the building. The church pews seating was rearranged and used for class room seating during school use. The black boards and etc. were brought into the room from storage area during school activities. There were only a couple of teachers who divided the grades 1-3 and 4-6 for clustering. The teacher moved from one grade to the other to teach while the other grades did special assignments. My teacher, Adelle Williams (Harris) was also a member of the church and a distant cousin. This made it impossible for anything that happened at school not to get back to my parents. When I reflect today on how limited my early exposure to education was and how it all ended up, it is simply amazing.

The teachers were methodical in their teaching and very devoted to their work, and gave us a good foundation. I often think about how much energy was displayed by these teachers to be sure that we got our lessons correct.

Junior and High School Experience

I was fortunate again to have knowledgeable, good and caring teachers. I did work hard and was able to excel in all of my subjects. My favorite subjects were math, science and public speaking. In later years, I was participating in plays and oratorical contests. I recall participating in speaking contests at school and traveling away to represent our school at district level competitions. I did go out for and made the football team one year. I played in two games the first year that I was on the team and it took all of my 115 lbs. to get through a couple of games. My size did not help me in this sport and since my interest was really in academics, it was a graceful way to give up on football after one year.

After graduating from Hale County Training School in Greensboro, Alabama with honors at age 16, it was off to college for me. My high school (although segregated) prepared me very well for college. I could write well, speak correctly and understood mathematics and science thoroughly. My high school teachers were all serious about our preparation and I do credit them for their care and concern during those developing years. I remember Mrs. Jackson in English and Ms. Hope in math to name a few who helped me get a good solid foundation in high school.

University/College Experience

I made application to only one university/college — Tuskegee Institute— because it was the only college/university that I wanted to attend. I was greatly impressed at age 15 when I had the opportunity to participate in a public speaking contest at Tuskegee Institute (now Tuskegee University) and to tour that beautiful and spacious campus. Dr. Booker T. Washington who founded the university had great vision about education, the development of each student and a very methodical layout of the physical plant. The big spacious campus of 1000 acres and over 100 buildings swept me from my feet and I was so impressed with it all.

History of Tuskegee University

Tuskegee University's slogan is "the pride of the swift, growing south." Founded in a one room shanty, near Butler Chapel AME Zion Church, thirty adults represented the first class - Dr. Booker T. Washington the first teacher. The founding date was July 4, 1881, authorized by House Bill 165.

We should give credit to George Campbell, a former slave owner, and Lewis Adams, a former slave, tinsmith and community leader, for their roles in the founding of the University. Adams had not had a day of formal education but could read and write. In addition to being a tinsmith, he was also a shoemaker and harness-maker. And he could have been experienced in other trades. W. F. Foster was a candidate for re-election to the Alabama Senate and approached Lewis Adams about the support of African-Americans in Macon County.

What would Adams want, Foster asked, in exchange for his (Adams) securing the black vote for him (Foster). Adams could well have asked for money, secured the support of blacks voters and life would have gone on as usual. But he didn't. Instead, Adams told Foster he wanted an educational institution — a school — for his people. Col. Foster carried out his promise and with the assistance of his colleague in the House of Representatives, Arthur L. Brooks, legislation was passed for the establishment of a "Negro Normal School in Tuskegee."

A $2,000 appropriation, for teachers' salaries, was authorized by the legislation. Lewis Adams, Thomas Dryer, and M. B. Swanson formed the board of commissioners to get the school organized. There was no land, no buildings, no teachers only State legislation authorizing the school. George W. Campbell subsequently replaced Dryer as a commissioner. And it was Campbell, through his nephew, who sent word to Hampton Institute in Virginia looking for a teacher.

Booker T. Washington got the nod and he made the Lewis Adams dream happen. He was principal of the school from July 4, 1881, until his death in 1915. He was not 60 years old when he died. Initial space and building for the school was provided by Butler Chapel AME Zion Church not far from this present site. Not long after the founding, however, the campus was moved to "a 100 acre abandoned plantation" which became the nucleus of the present site.

Tuskegee rose to national prominence under the leadership of its founder, Dr. Washington, who headed the institution from 1881 until his death at age 59 in 1915. During his tenure, institutional independence was gained in 1892, again through legislation, when Tuskegee Normal and Industrial Institute was granted authority to act independent of the state of Alabama.

Dr. Washington, a highly skilled organizer and fund-raiser, was counsel to American Presidents, a strong advocate of Negro business, and instrumental in the development of educational institutions throughout the South. He maintained a lifelong devotion to his institution and to his home — the South. Dr. Washington is buried on the campus of Tuskegee University near the University Chapel.

Robert R. Moton was president of Tuskegee from 1915 to 1935. Under his leadership, the Tuskegee Veteran's Administration Hospital was created on land donated by the Institute. The Tuskegee V.A. Hospital, opened in 1923, was the first and only staffed by Black professionals. Dr. Moton was succeeded in 1935 by Dr. Frederick D. Patterson. Dr. Patterson oversaw the establishment of the School of Veterinary Medicine at Tuskegee. Today, nearly 75 percent of Black veterinarians in America are Tuskegee graduates.

Dr. Patterson also brought the Tuskegee Airmen flight training program to the Institute. The all-Black squadrons of Tuskegee Airmen were highly decorated World War II combat veterans and forerunners of the modern day Civil Rights Movement. Dr. Patterson is also credited with founding the United Negro College Fund, which to date has raised more than $1 billion for student aid. Dr. Luther H. Foster became president of Tuskegee Institute in 1953.

Dr. Foster led Tuskegee through the transformational years of the Civil Rights Movement. Student action, symbolized by student martyr and SNCC member Sammy Younge, as well as legal action represented by *Gomillion v. Lightfoot* (1960), attests to Tuskegee's involvement in The Movement.

The fifth resident, Dr. Benjamin F. Payton, began his tenure in 1981. Under his leadership, the Tuskegee University National Center for Bioethics in Research and Health Care and the Tuskegee Airmen National Historic Site were launched. The General Daniel "Chappie" James Center for Aerospace Science and Health Education was constructed — the largest athletic arena in the SIAC. The Kellogg Conference Center, one of 12 worldwide, was completed as a renovation and expansion of historic Dorothy Hall.

Tuskegee attained University status in 1985 and has since begun offering its first doctoral programs in integrative biosciences and materials science and engineering. The College of Business and Information Sciences was established and professionally accredited, and the College of Engineering, Architecture and Physical Sciences was expanded to include the only Aerospace Engineering department at an HBCU.

On November 1, 2010, Dr. Gilbert L. Rochon became the sixth president of Tuskegee University. I was fortunate to lead the Board of Trustees steering committee in this selection. Dr. Rochon has held key positions in education, health, community and national agencies. He has an extensive background in international research and has put in place a robust agenda for the future of the university and its continued partnerships and collaborations with government, corporate and private industry. As Chairman of the Board of Trustees, I am committed to helping Dr. Rochon continue the legacy of Tuskegee University.

At the time of Washington's death, there were 1,500 students, a $2 million endowment, 40 trades, (we would call them majors today), 100 fully-equipped buildings, and about 200 faculty. From 30 adult students in a one room shanty, we have today grown to more than 3,000 students on a campus (the main campus, farm and forest land) that includes some 5,000 acres and more than 70 buildings.

Dedicated in 1922, the Booker T. Washington Monument, called "Lifting the Veil," stands at the center of campus. The inscription at its base reads, "He lifted the veil of ignorance from his people and pointed the way to progress through education and industry." For Tuskegee, the process of unveiling is continuous and lifelong.

University Mission

Tuskegee University is a national, independent, and state-related institution of higher learning that is located in the State of Alabama. The University has distinctive strengths in the sciences, architecture, business, engineering, health, and other professions, all structured on solid foundations in the liberal arts. In addition, the University's programs focus on nurturing the development of high-order intellectual and moral qualities among students and stress the connection between education and the highly trained leadership Americans need in general, especially for the work force of the 21st Century and beyond. The results we seek are students whose technical, scientific, and professional prowess has been not only rigorously honed, but also sensitively oriented in ways that produce public-spirited graduates who are both competent and morally committed to public service with integrity and excellence.

The University is rooted in a history of successfully educating African Americans to understand themselves and their society against the background of their total cultural heritage and the promise of their individual and collective future. The most important of the people we serve are our students. Our overall purpose is to nurture and challenge them to grow to their fullest potential. Serving their needs is the principal reason for our existence. A major outcome we seek is to prepare them to play effective professional and leadership roles in society and to become productive citizens in the national and world community. Tuskegee University continues to be dedicated to these broad aims.

Over the past century, various social and historical changes have transformed this institution into a comprehensive and diverse place of learning whose fundamental purpose is to develop leadership, knowledge, and service for a global society. Committed deeply to academic excellence, the University admits highly talented students of character and challenges them to reach their highest potential. The University also believes strongly in equality of opportunity and recognizes that exquisite talent is often hidden in students whose finest development requires unusual educational, personal, and financial reinforcement. The University actively invites a diversity of talented students, staff, and faculty from all racial, religious, and ethnic backgrounds to participate in this educational enterprise.

End

I started as a work student during the summer to supplement the funds necessary to enter in the fall. This work plan required a student to spend five (5) years at the university to secure a four year program. I worked as a janitor cleaning the dormitories, fireman for the furnaces, switch board operator and finally for the last two years, I was selected to participate in the undergraduate research program. My research area was in Biology and as a result, I was a laboratory assistant (I really watch over the lab) for Biology students in the freshman and sophomore levels. I thought a Doctor of Veterinary Medicine degree was best for me when I left home for school but changed my major in the second year to science and mathematics (these subjects were always my long suits).

I enrolled in and thoroughly enjoyed the Reserve Officer Training Corps (ROTC). I was impressed the legacy it represented and developed a passion for the military "spit and polish." I became commander of the highly regarded drill team; earned a distinguished military student designation at ROTC summer camp, and joined the Pershing Rifles Military Fraternity. Everyone on campus knew that I loved the military.

As a ROTC cadet at Tuskegee I became a member of The National Society of Pershing Rifles, the nation's premier undergraduate military fraternal organization. The Pershing Rifles organization emphasizes esprit de corps, motivation, and basic military skills. Its members were experts at unarmed, armed, and exhibition drill, and were the pride of the battalion and the college. Membership was considered a high military honor. The Pershing Rifles as a national organization was comprised of nearly 200 units stationed at ROTC detachments around the country. The Pershing Rifles were true to their basic purpose: to develop the traits of leadership and discipline among their members. My Road, which started along a path of faith and promise had opened up to a road leading to two significant pillars that would become milestones in my future development; Tuskegee University with its illustrious history of producing leaders in business, science, the military and education, and the U.S. Army, the pathway to achievement growth and service.

In the lab at Tuskegee.

The Pershing Rifles drill team was not just another drill team, it was considered one of the school's top entertainments and it participated regularly and often won several competitive events in the region. It was an added attraction at homecoming parades, football game and other school wide events. The team members were carefully selected and practices were thorough and disciplined. I was one of the longest serving drill team commanders when I graduated.

I did sustain an accident during my junior year while returning from my part-time job one evening. As I entered in the dormitory, a large crowd of students were in the hallway and were rushing toward the door that I came through. I remember having a coke (in a bottle) in my left hand and as I turned to go back through the door ahead of the crowd. I slashed my hand through the upper half of the door which was glass and cut my left wrist very bad. I was hospitalized for several weeks, got behind in my studies and suffered much agony in the healing process. I actually was prepared at one point to drop out of school and return home because of the big set-back in my academic work.

ROTC Drill Team.

I did get back on my feet and begin to put my academic work in order and prepare for Reserve Officer Training Corps (ROTC) summer camp. The preparation was tough going and I had to strengthen my arm and wrist and get into top shape to take on the rigorous training. This military summer camp was at Ft. Benning, Georgia and was the final test of one's ROTC training prior to receiving a commission. Although my wrist was still weak, I got through the training with an outstanding evaluation and was designated a distinguished military graduate.

Finding My Wife

Marjorie Seymore was the lovely young lady who came into my life while we were students at Tuskegee University. She was from North Carolina and was studying to become a nurse. We met at our freshman Halloween dance and I approached her for a dance. She politely rejected me. In order to minimize the obvious embarrassment, I extended an invitation to her friend who was with her and she accepted. We tried not to pay much attention to each other during the dance but it was difficult for me and probably for her as well.

We would see each other around the campus following that initial encounter and would always greet each other in a warm and friendly way. Both of us were thinking about this and began a slow relationship that was centered around some studying together and general conversations. It was clear from these encounters that there was a deeper interest and a level of compatibility was in place. From these meetings our relationship began to change and it grew and grew through the years at Tuskegee. We were engaged and she made visits to meet my family and I did the same visiting and being introduced to her family during the school breaks. We were very good friends who trusted and loved each other very much. My entire family became very fond of her and she felt the same about them. She had a wonderful family and they made me feel very comfortable as well.

During our four years of dating or "checking" as we called it at Tuskegee, both of us changed our majors. I changed from Pre-Veterinary medicine to Biology and Mathematics and Marjorie changed from Nursing to Home Economics. She wanted very much to be a teacher and I was looking at an Army career or medicine. What did not change was the way we felt about each other. Our plans were to marry during the summer following our graduation. It was one of our best decisions.

A Favorite Seat.

The directions of my career began to come into focus as I graduated on time with a B.S. degree and was commissioned as Second Lieutenant in the U.S. Army. This was one of the happiest and most enjoyable occasions that I had witnessed at this point in my life. All of my family which included my father and aunt made the journey to the campus to witness the first siblings of our family to receive a college degree. My future wife's family (father mother and two young sisters) were also there to share with us in the excitement. Since my last name was Williams, I thought it took a lifetime for them to get to my name that day. There were many smiles and some tears when my name was finally called and I walked across the stage receiving my Army Commission first, to be followed by receipt of my B.S. degree. This was a real treat and great day for my father who did shed a small tear. I had a strange but great feeling on that beautiful green lawn that mid May afternoon. It was a feeling I had not felt before and one that I have not felt afterwards. This was a new beginning and a significant milestone in my life. As I reflected for a few minutes on the path that I had traveled to get to this point in my life, I glanced to the sky and thought this could only happen in America. I felt like the luckiest person in the world. I knew at this point that I was traveling my own "road" and the only thing that I had to do going forward was to watch the sign posts, keep the faith, stay the course, and everything would be alright.

After the graduation ceremony there was a little refreshment and some small parties to rejoice over the long five years, but my focus quickly turned to the career ahead. I knew that I had just a short time to clean up my campus chores (checking out of the dorm, turning in the supplies, and etc) and go home to make a quick visit with the family and to get that special hug from my great grandmother. While she was unable to make the journey to witness my graduation ceremony, not because she was ill or approaching 100 years but that she loved her place and really didn't enjoy riding in automobiles and taking long trips. She was standing on her porch when I arrived home after college with my degree rolled in my hand and a big wide smile on my face, saying loudly and before we embraced, "Bannie, I did this just like you told me to do, and I have graduated from college on time." Then, the big hug came. I will never forget her quiet whisper in my ear saying, "My boy, I am proud of you and I knew you could do it."

On my way to my first duty station (Ft. Belvoir, VA) a few days later, I stopped over in North Carolina at my future wife's home to handle some of the administrative actions prior to marriage. My future in-laws were very nice people, and the family accepted me as their own and I gain great respect for them. After this short but important visit, I knew my "road" was headed in the right direction and the task for me at that time was to pay attention to this big sign post and navigate with care as I enter onto the delicate highway of marriage and family life.

Three

Starting the Career

Good character is the quality that makes one dependable whether being watched or not. —Franklin P. Adams

Army Officer (Engineer)

After an overnight bus ride from North Carolina to Washington, D.C., I reported into Ft. Belvoir, VA for active duty the next day (July 10, 1960) at around 11:00 A.M. This was a very exciting day for me to walk into an active duty setting for my initial training as a new Engineer officer in the U.S. Army. The academic and physical training of the course were equally challenging and required everyone to be at their best game. I worked hard and did very well in all parts of the course. After one month into the basic course, I took off a long weekend to return to North Carolina to get married. The wedding date (August 6, 1960) was set prior to us leaving college after receiving my active duty reporting date. Everything worked out as planned and my career and family were started at the same time. This was truly a big day for us. We had so much trust and confidence in each other.

The Big Day.

Our First Car
(My First Big Mistake)

We were excited after arriving in Washington, D.C. and finding a nice family (the Browns) who had a portion of their home to lease. All was in order except transportation for us to get around and for me to get to and from Ft. Belvoir, Virginia each day for school. We discussed the idea of purchasing a car and set out to begin to look for one during the afternoons as I came home from school.

I visited one used car lot and to make the story short – I arranged to purchase a car. It was a 1959 Bonneville Pontiac and was very big and attractive. As I was driving home to show this to my new wife, I began to feel that there was a problem. As soon as my wife saw it, she sat inside and asked what did it cost and as I tried to explain, she stated firmly that "this car is too expensive, too big and you must take it back." I went back to the dealer and he smiled as I went in to see him and said, "Lieutenant, you have bought this car and signed a contract, so I cannot take it back." I realized this was my first big mistake and one that I will never forget. Today, we laugh and use it as our examples of what not to do as we talk to our children and grand children. What a lesson!

My first duty assignment as a young engineer officer was with the 70th Engineer Battalion located at Ft. Campbell, Kentucky. It was a strange first exposure to my initial organization in that the entire organization (which included my battalion) was engaged in field training. I reported and signed into the organization and was immediately informed that the unit expected me to join them at the field training site. I had left my young wife at the guest house and had to return there to pick up a few things for the field, but most of all to inform her that I would be gone for a few days. As it would be, I stayed for fourteen days prior to returning. My wife had found a way (with the help of a nice lady she met at the guest house) to sign for and move into government housing. I will always remember this big job and how well she handled it alone.

First Car.

The fourteen days in a field training environment gave me the best orientation that a new officer could have. I was ready to be productive when we returned to our post. I often used this example of orientation with many junior officers through the years.

My initial duty assignment was an Assistant Operations Officer with the specific responsibility for training. I learned the organizational structure and how the Battalion was organized and trained very well and in the early stage of my first assignment. It was not long before I was thrust into a big job for my time in the Army, experience and rank. One of our companies (approx. 150 soldiers) became in need of a commander on a very short notice. I was tapped to fill this position which was two grades higher than my grade and experience. I was fortunate to be greeted by a very muscular first sergeant who had been around for awhile. He had wrestled as a younger man and his biceps were as large as my thighs – what a man! His name was Collier and his patience with me as a young green officer was remarkable. Sgt. Collier was direct and blunt with his words but was one of the best soldiers I have ever seen. He gets much of the credit for steering and getting my career started on the right foot. He would always give me his views and it was here that I learned to be a leader, it required steeped knowledge about your job. His commands to the troops were direct but loud and firm – when Sgt. Collier spoke everyone listened including me. I recall that he always wanted do a thorough job of investigating a situation prior to the young commander getting close to the issue He wanted me to always have good facts so I could deal professionally with the issues. He taught me so much of the practical side of being a soldier. We served a year and half together and became one of the best leadership teams in the Battalion.

There were many situations to write about during this command tour. The one or two that stand out as lessons learned centered on a month and a half field training exercise that took place 5-6 months after I took command. This unique training event required the entire Engineer Group to mobilize from Ft. Campbell, Kentucky to the vicinity of Sumter, South Carolina to participate in a massive river crossing operations which was part of a Corps size training exercise called "swift strike." We were required to construct bridges in multiple sites across the river in a designated time frame. This was taxing but very good training for all the elements of the organization. The training across the board was superb as it allowed us to operate in simulated war time conditions (including night operations). The travel time down and back to South Carolina consumed several days each way and a tremendous amount of travel time. We made several stops along the way for overnight stays and to perform some minor maintenance on the vehicles.

This training offered an opportunity for a young commander like me to have an opportunity to practice command and control and all that went along with it. It was also a unique experience to travel in a controlled convey through the small southern towns in 1961 as a black officer. All went well in this regard in spite of the strange looks I received along the way because full integration was just beginning to take hold. This was a major sign post on "My Road" as I was getting my Army career started.

My First Command.

Operation Swift Strike.

Flight School & Germany Assignment

Hold fast to dreams for if dreams die, life is a broken-winged bird that cannot fly.

—*Langston Hughes*

I applied for flight school toward the end of my tour at Ft. Campbell and passed all the examinations and tests and was accepted for aviation training as an Army pilot. The training site was in lower Alabama near the town of Ozark (Ft. Rucker) and it had been labeled as a tough training environment and that was a fact. I studied hard and learned the principles of flying an aircraft very quickly. While I completed every flight requirement tasks on time or ahead of time with good evaluations. It was truly a very difficult training environment for other reasons. This training was started in 1962 and the social/equality situation in this part of Alabama was not the best for African Americans at that time. While the school and most instructors tried to do the right thing in respect to fairness, there were still some issues existing and unfortunately my initial flight instructor was not over the segregated and bias mind-set. We sort of agreed thru body language to just coexist and spend the minimum amount of time interacting one-on-one. It was a very strange event that occurred on my first evaluation flight. He scored me prior to this evaluation at a grade of 70 and was absolutely shocked when my evaluation flight was over, the evaluation instructor scored me with one of highest evaluation of anyone in the class for that phase of our training. This was very difficult for him to understand and get over and it was clear to me that he was internalizing about his own mind-set regarding the qualifications and capabilities of a person of my race. We only had a few conversations subsequent to this event, and I soon moved to the next phase of training, and that was now behind both him and me. It was ironic through all this that he was very quiet and the supervising staff was quite upset over this disparity between his recommended score and my evaluation score. They offered me as mitigation for this situation the opportunity to switch instructors, but I refused because I felt it was time to not walk away from a situation but for everyone to learn to live and to understand that there is bias and we still have to work together, be fair and live through.

While this whole experience was somewhat unpleasant for me, Mr. Smith (my instructor) was unable to get over the fact that I received such high score on the first evaluation flight in the primary phase of my flight training. I believe deep within he knew that I could fly and fly very well, and it was the reality that took control of him. It goes without saying that this encounter was a big road sign along "My Road." My two colleagues who were on the same instructor team with me did not say much about him or the situation, but I knew it was a significant indication to them as to how unlevel the playing field was for me.

I came away from this experience in flight school fully armed with the fact that the "storm was not over" and there was much more work for our country to do in spite of all of Martin Luther King, Jr.'s effort. Again, another very valuable experienced in my career at age 24. After graduating from flight school with good grades/evaluations, it was off to my initial assignment as a pilot in Germany with a young wife, one child (a daughter – Patty) and our few possessions.

Home from flight training.

This experience of traveling from New York to Germany on a very large ship (The Buckner) was very exciting for our young daughter and me but not good for my wife as she was pregnant with our second child and was a little sick during the entire trip. She never let me forget how terrible this trip was for her but we made it together. We docked in Bremen, Germany, took an overnight train down to Hanau, Germany, near Frankfurt, and were met by my new boss and his wife; Captain Jim Tillman and his wife, Louise. It was great to finally get on the ground in Germany.

There was not sufficient military housing on base so we were directed to some very nice accommodations on the German economy. We were fortunate to find a duplex apartment that had one bedroom, a small living room, a kitchen, a bath and a sun porch. It was very nicely appointed and had a beautiful view of the countryside. Our young daughter loved to play in the yard and it was a very peaceful setting. Our landlady spoke very little English and our German was quite sparse, but we all became fast friends. Our stay only lasted ninety days, but our friendship lasted for years. She became very attached to our daughter and she cried when we had to move back to the base.

We got settled into housing and our three year tour of duty started. I was assigned to the 37th Engineer Group as an Aviator rather than as an Engineer because all new pilots had to spend the initial assignment after flight school in a flying job. I was lucky to be with the Engineers and was able to stay current with my branch counterparts and specialty. The flight duties to support this large Engineer unit kept the four aviators busy and away from home frequently.

The weather in central Germany at that time was always somewhat of a problem and we were required to fly in some pretty tough weather conditions. Since I had gone to fixed wing aviation training and had an instrument rating, I was able to cope with the weather better than my colleagues who were not instrument rated. I had my first small accident while supporting a field exercise around Giessen, Germany. I was making a simulated mail pick up in a field and was not able to get enough carburetor heat to the engine in time for landing. I lost power in the turn to the final approach and had to put the aircraft down using proper emergency procedures. The aircraft (OIA) sustained only minor damage and I was lucky to have no injuries. Given the circumstances, this was a good outcome although, I was very embarrassed over the whole matter. I soon put it behind me and was cleared to fly again in a few days.

The other very tough weather challenge was flying in and out of Wildflecken Germany where we had a battalion to support. It appeared that there was a mission to fly to Wildflecken almost every day. The location was at a very high elevation and almost each flight we were in and out of the clouds. In a nutshell, it was a tough flight assignment to this location. Even landing on the sloping runway was a challenge for every fixed wing aviator. It was an old aviator saying that "if you could fly in Germany in the winter, you could fly anywhere in the world."

After a year and a half, I became an instructor pilot in the Beever (U8) aircraft and provided this service for our unit. This was a delicate additional duty in that I had to administer flight evaluation to my supervisor and peers alike and remain current myself. As instructor pilot, I was required to fly the airplane from the right seat rather than the left and this was a challenge and required much skill and practice. We had only one of this aircraft type assigned and it was busy all the time because it could handle a passenger load of 4-5 passengers. It was also very good for longer trips due to the fuel on board capacity and general durability of the airplane.

Marjorie made friends and was able to cope with my long temporary duty assignments. Our second child and first son, Chuck, was born. This brought joy and more responsibility to us. We did save enough money to travel a bit in Europe and to get out and learn some of the German culture. We took a "drive it" vacation thru Southern Europe during our second summer in Germany. It was a terrific experience to say the least. We traveled on this first vacation to Southern Europe (Italy, Switzerland, and Austria). The entire trip was two weeks by car and rail.

I recall that the Army promotion list to Captain was released while we were traveling. I was eager to find a military instal at ion so I could purchase a copy of *Stars and Stripes* the official military newspaper. I had succeeded in being promoted. My wife and I celebrated the news.

Our third child, Calvin, was born toward the end of my tour in Germany, and only thirteen months behind his brother. This was another blessing for us and the family was set at age 26. We found a very nice German lady who would baby sit our children. I recall her name was Frau Wilke, and she rode her bike to our house each day regardless of the weather. She was so kind to my wife and children and as a result, we treated her as a member of the family and learned German from her as well. By getting to know this nice lady, we learned to appreciate the German culture, the country, and the people. This was our first lesson in how important it is to make an effort to study and learn another person's culture and language. This was a great experience for the entire family.

The war in Vietnam was heating up and the need for helicopter pilots was critical. As a result, I was tapped for more flight training (Helicopter training) and was issued orders to Vietnam for my next assignment. This was good and bad news as the opportunity to learn to fly helicopters was exciting but the notion of leaving my young family for a war zone was very tough for us. It was at this junction in many young aviators' careers when they begin to leave the Army. My boss, a Captain left the military to become a commercial pilot. Two of my flying colleagues got out of the Army and returned to civilian life. There were times when all of us did deep thinking about the future in respect to careers and etc. My wife and I discussed in much detail the idea of departing the Army as well, but made the decision to stay with it for the following reasons:

- Both of us were beginning to like the Army life

- I was doing very well with my development and advancement (i.e. I had received my regular Army designation while in Germany). My wife had adjusted well to Army life and was a very supportive partner.

- President John F. Kennedy (who we simply admired) had been assassinated while we were in Germany. This tragic event left us with a feeling of loss and a determined spirit to serve honorably in his memory. There was the sense of responsibility among us all to remember his words, "ask not what my county could do for me but what I could do for my country."

- Finally, my wife said to me that "you are a good Army engineer, an excellent aviator and an outstanding officer—go and serve in Vietnam—we will be OK."

It was a little awkward for me as it is for most pilots to transition from being an airplane (fixed wing) pilot to a helicopter pilot. There was a class consisting of about 30 pilots who had the same transitional problems so it was fun and this common issue made the transition smoothly. My wife and youngest son (Calvin) would come out to the airfield toward the end of the training day and watch me take off and land. It goes without saying that my family (father, grand-parents and etc) were not excited about this Vietnam assignment, but it was something I felt was a responsibility and service to my country. So, I felt okay about it.

Our youngest child needed some special medical care and that kept things somewhat unsettled for the family while I was going through helicopter transition training. Marjorie spent much of her time in and out of hospitals for tests, including Walter Reed in Washington, D.C., watching over our young son. We were thankful that the medical issue was now under control and we were assured that our son was fine prior to my departure for Vietnam. All of this made us stronger for the long separation and we often engage in reflections today on how this event framed our perspective. It was clear from this experience that things do not always happen at the best of times.

Williams' Family

Four

Vietnam War

Experience

The family was settled in North Carolina at my wife's family home and I was off to Vietnam to participate in the war as a helicopter pilot. Marjorie's mother was so kind to me and I felt relieved that she was there to help us with our young children. My wife went to work as a school teacher at the school she graduated from. We had a very stable and solid marriage. We decided to communicate through cassette tapes and the mail. I was so proud of Marjorie's strength and the devotion she displayed during this critical time. My assignment was with the 228th Assault Helicopter Company stationed in the middle of one of the most active war locations in Vietnam. Our organization was nick named "Tomahawks" and we had both troop carrying helicopter (slicks) and armed helicopters (gun-ships). After a few hours of in country orientation and a few take offs, landings and a few auto rotations, I was declared ready to begin flying regular missions. The helicopter skill set was so critical that only the minimum amount of time could be spent on orientation and tune up. The primary function of this unit was to airlift the fighting soldiers into the battle areas and extract them when the mission was finished. In order to accomplish this, the landing area had to be prep by our "gun-ships" and the route to and from of the battle area was under armed helicopter escort. It goes without saying that the helicopter offered a target of opportunity for the enemy and as a result, we were often attacked while we were delivering soldiers to the landing zone and similarly as we were extracting soldiers. These were very difficult missions that were required during both night and day and in all types of weather. It required skill and knowledge of the helicopter and also familiarity with the operating area. It was not unusual for pilots to fly 10 hours per day during the peak of a war operation. After three or four months of flying in-country, I was designated as a Command Pilot. This meant I could now fly from the left seat while a less experienced pilot would operate from the right seat of the cockpit. In a nutshell, I was the boss of the aircraft.

My assault helicopter company was staffed very well with seasoned and very experience aviators. I recall our company commander was a Lt. Colonel and the platoon commanders were Majors. The company also had a delicate and big mission supporting both the First Infantry and 25th Infantry divisions. Both of these big divisions were in the thick of the activity and fight in the 3rd U.S. Corps area. As stated, our flying missions were conducted both day and night even in marginal weather. This flying assignment required all to be at his best at all times and most of all to have a clear head and focus on the operations of the helicopter and the mission.

As a result of the support mission my unit was assigned. We participated in the entire major operations in that battle area during this tour. I recall participating in a very difficult mission that occurred one night when we were required to fly without lights. It was a total blackout mission. Since all our flights to and from insertion or extraction missions were always conducted in formation, this evening was no exception. The mission was so delicate that it required us to fly the most experienced pilots in the organization. As a result in many cases, there were instructor pilots, and command pilots in the same cockpit. It was a long flight to the activity area and it was in the late evening. The mission was to extract a battalion size unit (400-500 soldiers) that had been fighting in an area that was under heavy fire. It was pretty tough going for us as almost every aircraft was hit with fire as we made our descent into the area for the extractions. It was not a nice looking site on the ground and there were casualties and active fighting activity all over the area. I think each helicopter made three sorties into and out of this tough area that evening and completed the mission. This was without question an evening that I shall never forget. I saw too many tears and heard too many groans. It was finally over and the long flight back to our base camp was a time for the crew to talk and think about this war and to conclude that it may be described many ways but one thing was crystal clear, it was not pretty.

We lived in what was called hooches with two persons in a hooch and each with his own mosquito net over the bed. There was very little privacy in the hooches and our showers were outside in a gang type arrangement where four or five persons would shower at the same time. Our cafeteria (mess hall) was a little walk from the hooches but the food was plentiful and generally good. There was very little spare time to spend on down time and relaxation so there was little need for any recreational type arrangements. While there was not much time for recreation, we did have a few facilities and equipment for that purpose.

Vietnam Hooche.

Almost every night there was either rocket or mortar fire in coming to our compound. We all had a space and designated bunkers below the ground to protect us from the mortars and rockets. While it was a routine event, it was an event that one could never get use to, and an experience that I could never forget. I made a small tape or wrote a short letter each day to keep my family full abreast as to what was going on with me and gave them a general update on the war. My wife also wrote almost every day as well to keep me informed on how they were doing back at home. Since our unit was in the thick of the fight, we had aircrafts shot up and shot down periodically and we lost pilots and some sustained serious injuries. This was really war!

We were very busy and had very little time off in as much we worked seven days each week. There was one 5-7 day rest and recuperation (R&R) for each of us at the 6 month mark in a 12 month tour.

I selected Hawaii for my R&R, and arranged for my wife to meet me there. This allowed me a break from the daily grind of the war, an opportunity to see my wife, and to relax for a few days. This was good for both of us because "war" and the absence of normal life wears on both of us. I am so proud of how my wife coped with all the time I had to be away. After flying as a command pilot and serving as section leader for about nine months of my twelve month tour, I was assigned as the base development officer for the company. This was an unusual assignment for an aviator in a war zone but a great one for an engineer officer. I had flown so many hours on this tour and since this assignment was ideal for me, I was pleased. My responsibility covered the entire base camp operations for my unit. This job required me to supervise the local Vietnamese labor force, the maintenance and new construction of some additional facilities to the camp. It was an exciting and busy job for the last three month of my tour. In this job, I was also required to fly on a mission by mission basis to fill in a crew slot so my flying continued but at a reduced level. In this capacity, I also handled all of the company's administration, logistics and support activities.

I recall on a very quiet Sunday afternoon, our company was called to support what appeared to be a very simple insertion mission. The mission was to fly about 5 miles from our base camp to pick up some of South Vietnam soldiers and insert them in an area where the Viet Kong was suspected of hiding. I was tapped to fly as command pilot with a new major who had just a short time in country. To me, this was a simple mission and no big deal.

After we made the pickup and began to make the landing for the initial insertion, the attack started and was pretty intense for some minutes. When this activity started, we were into our decent for landing with soldiers aboard. As soon as we were about to touchdown, our helicopter was hit many times and I began to pull out of the landing zone, our aircraft received a hit in the fuel tank, and it was forced down. I was flying the aircraft and we were able to execute the entire emergency check for a 'force down' and we got down with only a hard landing. This was a situation that soldiers like us had all trained and prepared for, but no one looks forward to putting into action. We were down on the ground for about 15 minutes or so, although it seemed like hours. It was the first time I saw an enemy take a direct aim with his weapon at me and the helicopter. We had good Air Force coverage immediately and were extracted by another nearby troop carrying helicopter and I was fortunate to have only minor injuries. Our door gunner, Specialist McDonald, performed extremely well during this difficult situation. This first tour of duty was a very long and busy year that ended with me logging over 1500 hours of flight time, receiving over 20 Air medals, the award of the Distinguished Flying Cross and Vietnamese Cross of Gallantry with a Silver Star. It was without question one of the busiest and loneliest years of my life.

Ready for another flight in the fight.

The UH-1 - Huey, the workhorse in Vietnam.

My Impression

I left Vietnam to come home from that terrible war with a very clear picture about values and how important it was to learn how to work as a team and appreciate the views of your fellow man. War is a barometer of one's ability to endure and will test any person's will to work together in order to survive. I saw conditions that I could not imagine and people simply working it out one situation at a time. I witnessed a grown man cry openly for the first time – not just a few tears but really cry out. My returning home to see my family and attend the Advanced Engineer Officer's Course was great, but I had received orders prior to leaving Vietnam that a second tour would follow after school. This news left me fully aware that nothing about war is pleasant… war is war! The important "take away" from this experience was the absolute necessity to insure that there is a good understanding as to why there was war and what we were trying to accomplish in the war. You cannot teach this in the heat of the battle … I believe it must be cemented in the mind-set of all who are asked to serve prior to entering the war zone. We purchased our first home in North Carolina near my wife's family. It was a good decision since it gave us privacy as a family and was close enough to my in-laws that they could help my wife with their grandchildren. Marjorie was fortunate to find a teaching job at the same school that she had attended growing up. This was excellent as it provided an opportunity to return to her community as a professional educator and a product of the dedicated teachers that inspired her career choice. She enjoyed the experience very much and this was a good situation for us during the separation period.

I was promoted to Major while attending the Engineer Officers Advanced Course at Ft. Belvoir, Virginia. I decided not to relocate my family to Ft. Belvoir since I was headed back to Vietnam immediately after school. As a result of this decision, I had to commute on the weekends and bring Marjorie to Ft. Belvoir for special occasions. This arrangement was not good but is an example of one of the unpleasant aspects of war and serving our country. We understood both!

My second tour in Vietnam following my Advance Engineer Officers' Training was slightly different as I was now a Major rather than a Captain. I was again assigned to an Engineering unit as was the situation in Germany. Having just completed a year of training in advanced engineering concepts and tuning up academically, I returned for my second tour in Vietnam but this tour would be in the 2nd Corps sector. Since this was still Vietnam, this assignment was in a different area that required total familiarization and orientation. I cannot tell you how empty and without motivation this second tour was shaping up to be. It was unbelievably hard for me to leave my family so soon for this place again. It was hard because I knew too much about how it would be, once I arrived at my new location. It was tough to buy into this second tour, to say the least. The long flight from Travis Air Force Base in California to Guam before a stop for fuel provided too much time to think and rethink about so many subjects. It was a very strange feeling and the level of excitement was really not there.

I was assigned as aviation officer of the 18th Engineer Brigade, a very large theater wide heavy construction Brigade that had a huge geographical area to cover. The aviation section provided air transportation for the Brigade Headquarters using both airplanes and helicopters. I arrived at this new assignment as a very experienced aviator and immediately qualified and became an instructor pilot in the UH-1 helicopter. This was the same aircraft that I had flown the year during my first tour in Vietnam. This training also allowed me the opportunity to keep all of our pilots current and on occasions, I was able to help out other organizations located at our site. It was a good assignment for career development and the opportunity to stay very current in wartime engineering and construction. The responsibility of the Brigade covered a very large area and the work was equally interesting. I recall our Brigade constructing an assortment of buildings, asphalt roads, installing wells and construction of Base Operations Support facilities. The Brigade had a very good mission and a great reputation in the theater. I worked for two of the finest general officers that I knew (BG John Elder and BG John Morris). Both were colonels when they arrived in the Brigade and went on to be promoted further and became Lieutenant Generals. One of these generals was a West Point graduate and the other was commissioned through the R.O.T.C. at VMI. It was interesting to watch their styles and how they approached each challenge and situation. This was a great assignment!

This second tour was cut short somewhat at the ten month point due to an injury to my wife (she was badly burned on her arm) while cooking for our young children. After returning home from her job as a school teacher, she was preparing some french fries for the kids as a treat when a kitchen mishap caused a fire to erupt. She was able to get the children and our little pet dog (Skippy) out of the house without injury. The house was basically destroyed. In her effort to get everyone to safety and put the fire out, she was seriously burned. I will always love her for how she bravely delivered the children and our pet to safety and fought to save our home at the expense of being burned. She was taken to the local hospital. My in-laws, who lived nearby, took care of the children. Everyone was very helpful during this difficult period. The local fire department did the best they could to save the house, but was unsuccessful. The military system (Army, Air Force and U.S. Coast Guard) and the American Red Cross did a superb job of getting me out of Vietnam and back home in record time. This was a very difficult time for all of us. My wife received good medical care at the local hospital, later at the Walter Reed Army Medical Center and after much therapy, she recovered very well. It was a painful ride for all of us during the healing period but we work together and made it. Again, it was a defining experience that "war is war" and much comes with it and one can never forget the total wear and tear on a family. This war experience of two years made me a much stronger and caring person who developed a good clear outlook on life and the world. As a result, I have been able to keep everything in focus and balanced over the years as a result of these horrible experiences.

Skippy – Our pet.

Five

Starting the Climb

Graduate School

Having the opportunity to be selected for two years of graduate school to pursue a Masters of Business Administration (MBA) in the city of Atlanta was truly a reward. It was appropriate that my graduate schooling would be in business management, the location was excellent for my wife's rehabilitation and the schools for the children were decent as well. I was pleased that Marjorie could also take some graduate courses and after a few months was back into the classroom teaching Home Economics again at one of the newest high schools. Since this schooling was at the full expense of the U.S. Army, I had both a graduate school performance measure and a follow-on service requirement to satisfy after completion of my graduate schooling. It was a great experience to interact with my civilian counterparts and learn a lot and received a strong Masters of Business Administration (MBA) with a management focus. I recall studying the entire Christmas holidays for exams during my first year in graduate school. I was determined to do well in every course as I was the first fully funded Army officer student in a full-time status at this university.

I did find the time to get some hands-on training while in graduate school during my free time. This unique practical experience was with a manufacturing company and it was excellent to observe processes. I was able for the first time to see the value in executive line type management. While it was not known or emphasized at that time but, I really was exposed to the concept of "Lean Management." It was important to observe how this management team would watch the critical process modes and address problems from that point of view — great experience!

My MBA class was unique in that most of the students had experience in the private sector and the classroom instruction was spirited and knowledge based. The faculty was a mix of research professors and professionals who were practicing the trade. It was amazing how focused the students were and how we pushed the instructors on all fronts. We were fortunate to have very good instructors who really had an interest in our learning. The best description of me as a student was that of a sponge looking to soak up everything that came my way from classroom instruction and books. I wanted to learn the theory and practice of management very well. My academic program was packed with a full load of all the management and organizational behavior courses the school would allow. I took a full load each semester and still found a way to get some hands on experience as an intern at a local business during my off time. This extra work was not a requirement for my MBA but it was what I wanted in order to be able to practice immediately. This was truly a great training and academic exposure opportunity for me at this time in my career and a great time for the family as well. After two years, I graduated with honors and my management style began to come into focus as "My Road" continued.

Development of Management Style

The style that emerged was one that required the following:

- Take command of your responsibility area
- Write the basics of all presentations you give
- Speak from experience and your heart
- Be the smartest person in the room on your subject
- Be direct, correct with guidance and responses
- Scope out potential modes of failure early
- Accept and understand reality
- Always manage for results
- Keep a keen eye on how you rise to the top so that it will be easy if you had to take a step or two back
- Stay focused on the big issue and the desired result
- Know that management will not work well without good leadership
- Know that human capital is the best asset
- Looking constantly for new methods and means
- Change will require a delicate leadership touch

Military Schooling – Mid Level

Armed with my new MBA degree and two full years of graduate school under my belt, I was once again off to my next level of schooling. This phase of preparedness was my mid-level military schooling at the Command and General Staff College at Ft. Leavenworth, Kansas. This year at Ft. Leavenworth was often referred to as a tough academic year for a mid-level officer but regarded as one of the best years of an Army officer's military life.

The trip by car from Atlanta to Kansas was an exciting experience for the family. We arrived at Ft. Leavenworth, Kansas a bit early to get our on-post housing sorted out prior to the rest of the class arriving. We were assigned to housing on post that was smaller than we were living in at Atlanta and I believe it was called "sub-standard" and a splinter village. The living room of this two level barracks like building had a support column or as the children said "a pole in the middle of the living room." Since this housing was once a troop barracks with individual rooms and later converted to an apartment, the support column was left in place. We were really excited at the notion of being on post where we did not have to worry about the drive from Kansas City each day. Overtime, this housing began to look better each day when deep snows and cold winters arrived. I knew housing was assigned according to grade and since I was a junior major, this was the best I could claim. We made the best and enjoyed it.

This year was exciting in a number of ways as both my wife, children and I took lessons and learned to play golf. It turned out that I really started enjoying the game and could not stay off the course. The school sponsored a number of great events for the students. I recall there was a Christmas shopping event for the male students called "a king for a night." We were bused to the big shopping area in Kansas City in order to do our holiday shopping. It was good fun and again allowed for good interaction with some of the smartest officers in the Army. I can truly say that the year that my family and I spent at Ft. Leavenworth, Kansas was all it was advertised to be. I met some lasting friends and was exposed to outstanding instructors and many superb military officers. The many special lectures by senior visiting officers and our section discussions/exercises were the highlights. I learned all aspects of our Army very well from this unique training environment.

First Washington Assignment

My road continued after these three years in school. This academic preparation was very pivotal training in any Army Officer's career because by the selection to attend, it began to give one indications that the Army had plans for you going forward. It did not necessary suggested that you were tracking to become a general officer, but it did send a clear signal that you were on the right path for a very successful career. It prepares one for the tough and visible jobs in the Army going forward. It goes without saying that I was happy with all of this and looked forward to the follow-on assignment. After a very productive year at Ft. Leavenworth and graduating from the Command and General Staff College, I was reassigned to the Army Material Command in Washington, D.C. My specific assignment was a Management Analyst in the Office of the Comptroller. This assignment was a utilization assignment for the two years of graduate training that I had received at the Army's expense at Atlanta University. This assignment at the Army

Material Command headquarters was a good utilization assignment because this command operated very much like a very large fortune 500 business. In this assignment, I had an opportunity to be exposed to all aspects of Comptrollership to include, budget, front end analytical work, cost analysis, accounting and management. After about 18 months as a Management Analyst, I had the opportunity to work directly for a wonderful General Officer, BG. Leslie Sears. General Sears was the Comptroller of the Army Material Command and was a very direct and quick minded person with a great command of the numbers.

I was designated to serve in addition to my regular duties as his speech writer, where through this experience I had an opportunity to develop many analytical charts and graphs and frame out the narrative to support each. This was great experience to capture the whole picture in a presentation for a senior officer. It was here that after about year and a half that he saw enough of my work to recommend me to the Comptroller of the Army, Lt. General Kjelstrom, to be his Staff Assistant/Aide-D-Camp. In this capacity, working for this high profile senior officer on the Army staff, I had an opportunity to learn much as we traveled to every corner of the Army structure. It was a truly invaluable experience to watch him interact and deal with the aspects of his jobs that related to Comptrollership and proved to be a phenomenal lesson in leadership and management. It was simply fantastic to watch him work issues and arrive at a solution and path forward. I learned how to work a room and see everyone who was important in a very short time frame. This assignment offered many opportunities; one was the chance to meet many of the key people around the Army doing important work. I prepared trip reports and recorded significant observations and assisted the Comptroller of Army with his administrative duties.

The job was not an easy one by any stretch of imagination. I did have my ups and downs here with the workload and the adjustment to style and etc. In this capacity, I had to always be ahead of the principal in my thinking and planning in order to be prepared to respond to tasks and tough requirements. The office of the comptroller at that time was one of the pivotal elements on the Army staff and very few actions did not come our way for sign off. In addition to having functional oversight over all comptrollers servicing throughout the Army structure, the office also oversaw the Army finance center, and the Army Comptroller's MBA Program at Syracuse University to name a few. In a nutshell, this was a busy office and the job was tough to say the least. I did not do as well in this position as planned but what I learned was much about how the Army staff functioned and it was unmatched by any previous assignment. I really felt that whatever the task or assignment assigned to me going forward could not be any more difficult… and I was right! LT. General Kjelstrom did facilitate a good and suitable follow-on assignment for me which I will discuss in following paragraph.

After this job, I was assigned to the trenches as the Operations and Maintenance Budget Analyst because training was a very key and significant portfolio. This was a very interesting assignment/portfolio in that it contains all of the Army's training funds including the military academy and recruiting command. It also gave me the opportunity to see much of the training and to understand why our training budgets were critical to the Army's mission. This was a very interesting and stimulating job because it allowed me to be exposed to parts of the Army that I would have never seen in my normal engineer rotation of assignments. I had an opportunity to interact with all the operating elements on Army and the staff as well. This assignment was followed with an assignment as the Executive Officer to the O&M Director.

This was a great job because once again, I had an opportunity to see not only the training program dollars but all of the funding that supported every aspect of the Army from the Operations and Maintenance perspective. These series of assignments in the Comptroller of the Army's office were significant sign posts along my road. I spent several years in this follow-on assignment and always had a full plate of work. The one big plus of this very busy job was to learn how to staff an action, evaluate the input and comments that our staff presented on issues and programs. I was fascinated with how critical the man-power and Base Operations funding was to the Army's operations and maintenance effort. I recall that both areas had strong and very knowledgeable leaders and managers during my tenure in the organization.

Battalion Command Assignment

After being promoted to Lt. Colonel and selected for Battalion Command soon thereafter, I handed over my responsibilities to a replacement and I was off to Ft. Belvoir, VA to take command of an Engineer training battalion. This command assignment was the dream of every Lt. Colonel and was a good signal that the Army still had a future plan for you. This assignment location was very significant to me and my family since it was the location of my first active duty station. This command assignment was in the training environment at the United States Army Engineers School, Ft. Belvoir, VA. My battalion consisted of four companies and was a mix of officers (basics and advanced) and some specialized enlisted students from all of the services. This was an excellent opportunity for me to see the level of talent my branch of service was producing and sending to the field. I recall that in addition to my command duties, each senior commander was encouraged to participate in the installation community activities. I chose to coach little league football and basketball. This was a wonderful experience and the opportunity to coach our youngest son since his age matched the coaching vacancy that I took. Our team won the championship for our region and age group one year and was competitive each year that we were stationed there.

Battalion change of command.

The battalion had field training requirements for the student that ranged from map reading, river crossings exercise and demolition training. It was all very interesting and excellent to keep me up and fresh on the level of training that our officers and enlisted personnel were receiving prior to going to new assignments. One of the most interesting aspects of this command assignment was to interaction with about a dozen foreign officers from several countries. All of these officers were in the United States for Military Engineering Training and returning back to their countries. In another part of the battalion, we had servicemen/women from other services. The importance of this command for me was to see every aspect of Military Engineering and some of the personnel who I would be working with in the future. It was great exposure and a wonderful opportunity to continue to grow and develop in leadership and management. Since my battalion was populated with officers and enlisted men/women in training, I was invited on a regular basis to visit and sit in on any and all training if time permitted. This gave me an opportunity to become very current on all aspects of military engineering and related subjects. The requirements for my wife's participation were many and she balanced these duties exceptionally well and held a full-time teaching job. I did well in this command assignment and was selected to remain at Ft. Belvoir as the Deputy Brigade Commander of a newly activated training Brigade. This was a great experience to work at the cutting edge of a newly activated organization and work thru all of the start-up challenges. I was selected for early promotion to Colonel and the War College, so I left early from the Training Brigade to attend the Army War College. This was another significant sign post on "My Road."

Six

Entering into the Fast Lane

Army War College

A selection for attendance to the War College was clearly an indication that all was okay so far with your career and that the future was generally bright. I was very pleased with this opportunity and took full advantage of all the learning opportunities offered during the full year of study. We were divided into seminars and work groups to facilitate close interaction and maximum learning. We were exposed to lectures/speeches from the top government and private sector executives. It was truly a memorable year that prepared me well for the senior assignments that followed. I was fortunate to be selected as an adjunct member of the current affairs panel for my college class. This panel made trips to universities, civic organizations and other activities to tell the Army's story. It was outstanding in every way and I enjoyed it very much.

Our class (1980) was a very large class by comparison and in my view had some of the Army's best officers. This was verified by the number of General Officers this class year 1980 produced. The class consisted of a dozen or so Foreign Service, other Government agencies students. It was truly a good mix and the section arrangement for the class work was stimulating and facilitated great interest. Each student had to do research and write a paper on a region of the world and a management area. I chose Western Europe and specifically Germany as my area of concentration. I was particularly interested in the German culture and behaviors before and after the World War II event as a comparison. My management topic was centered on installation management and how it could impact the quality of life and troop morale going forward. Both research areas were stimulating and exciting projects to work with. Since these were major assignments, much time and thought went into the preparation and presentation. I was able to use all of my hard work on the paper in my follow-on Brigade and Community Command assignment. As a community commander (installation commander) in Germany, this became a great laboratory to use all of the concepts and approaches explored in the papers — A great learning experience!

Our class, as all those before us, made the trip to New York City to gain both political and economical first-hand knowledge. It was great exposure that allowed us to interact at new levels of business and government and visit the United Nations and Wall Street. It was a well organized trip and utilized our time very well. We heard presentations and lectures from the active Army, the reserves, and the other services' senior officers. They were designed to keep us in tight with the moving parts of the military as we were away during this one year period. The post, in Carlisle Barracks, PA, was a delightful place for families as all of us enjoyed the many activities available. During this year away from the fast-paced routine in my duty assignment, I was able to reflect and look at "My Road" so far and think about where it could go, as I was beginning to like what I was seeing.

While attending the Army War College, I was selected for Brigade level command and an assignment as Brigade Commander of the 18th Engineer Brigade in Karlsruhe Germany. Prior to connecting to my command assignment, I had a one year assignment which took me back to the Pentagon with an assignment as Assistant Chief of Engineers' (ACE) office. I was responsible for the Installation Management Division and it was the perfect fit for me. I was fresh from the War College, had written my paper on Installation Management and all that was in that lane. This assignment also offered me an opportunity to learn and work on some mobilization requirements and general facilities issues. All of this was very valuable as I was also preparing for my brigade command. I was promoted to Colonel in this assignment and it was a happy occasion in as much as I had been on the promotion list for over a year. The officer who officiated was BG Sam Kem, a fine officer that I learned to admire and respect. It was time to begin attending the senior of pre-command courses and head to Germany.

On October 21, 1977 the 18th Engineer Brigade was reactivated at Karlsruhe, Germany. For the next 15 years, the Brigade served as the principal construction brigade for the United States Army Europe and 7th Army. During this period, the Brigade performed numerous construction, rehabilitation and renovation missions in military communities and training areas throughout USAREUR. Most noteworthy were the massive range upgrade of the Grafenwoehr Major Training Area in the early 1980's, and the construction of the Range 23 complex at the Wildflecken Major Training Area in 1989 and 1990. Additionally, the Brigade was responsible for providing topographic support to the European Theater.

Brigade Change of Command in Germany.

Brigade Command Experience

The 18th Brigade was not just another colonel level command but a special command that had produced a string of General Officers. It was the same Brigade I had served with in Vietnam as a Major and was highly sought after by all engineer colonel selectees. This move to Germany was not as easy on my family as in previous years. Our daughter was in her second year of college at University of Virginia, both sons were in high school which included one as a class officer and both were playing sports as starters. We were finally able to get everyone settled down and I was off to pre-command training for this assignment. I left my wife to clean up the loose ends with schools and etc., and I do thank her today for this important job.

After completing all the pre-command training and the family joining me in Germany, we were ready for a three year tour in the best job in the Army. The Brigade had a big and exciting mission and was at that time the largest heavy Engineer Brigade in the active Army. In addition to serving as Brigade Commander, I was also the Karlsruhe Community Commander, i.e. the equivalent of a small town mayor. This additional responsibility had a separate reporting channel and a separate staff. It was through this organization that most of my work and interaction with the German economy took place. The workload was particularly complex given the issues and concerns ranging from transportation, housing, medical, recreation, logistics, administration, schools and police issues.

This brigade being the largest in the Army structure at that time required a full colonel as my deputy. I was fortunate to have COL Dan Clark at the beginning and COL Dick Miles at the end of my tour to manage the day to day program. Both of these colonels were outstanding and did a great job handling the rear while I was away at Graf with the range construction project. Dan and his wife Kathy met me at the airport upon my initial arrival to the command and Dick and his wife, Faye, insured that we had a nice send off when my tour was finished.

This dual command arrangement required a very delicate balance of my time. I was able to get my balance and made a quick transition and started the journey in pretty good shape. The brigade had a large theater construction responsibility and also had been designated to lead the massive upgrade of the NATO Firing ranges for (tank) armored fighting vehicles training in Germany. This task would require all of the heavy Engineer troops capabilities stationed in Germany to do this mission. The number of soldiers to be involved soon grew to over 3700 and hundreds of pieces of equipment. This would be the largest troop construction project since World War II.

Re-building the Tank Ranges

This was without question a daunting task for any organization but the thought of doing these delicate upgrades with soldiers (troops) made it even more interesting. We planned well and trained up the organization to do this work and mobilized from many corners of West Germany to the training site at Grafenwohr Germany. This was a very large task force that consisted of both operational and support activities.

It was important to repeat that this brigade (the 18th Engineer Brigade) was the largest heavy construction unit in the active U.S. Army at that time and the leadership of this organization was sought after by many aspiring colonels. This command had produced a string of General Officers and was widely recognized as one of the best assignments. I think it is appropriate to mention that there was a little opposition to me being designated as Brigade Commander of this command. I had heard this was going on prior to my departing from the United States for the job. My selection was breaking a long list of commanders who were United States Military Academy graduates, and I was the first African American to lead this organization. It was my understanding that General Fritz Kroesen, commander of all Army forces in USAREUR (United States Army Europe) heard about this chatter and immediately closed it down. I might add that General Kroesen was very supportive of me from the day I started my command tour until he departed the command. He was a true professional and one of the fairest persons I have ever known, a great leader, a true professional and mentor. I recall that one of our big tasks was to rebuild about eleven NATO tank ranges such that they could accommodate the training requirements for the new M-1 tank family of fighting vehicles. This massive range modernization project was high profile and required us to build on each range a small staging compound and a state-of-the-art firing range that featured pop up targets, moving targets and "run lanes,"etc. The construction duration was short for each phase due to the need for the range for training.

Starting the construction.

The Range Modernization Project

The command, United States Army Europe (USAREUR) had determined that the existing ranges could not support the advance weaponry (M-1 tank) and the associated training requirements for fighting armored vehicles. The 18th Engineer Brigade was designated to lead this massive modernization effort. As the new commander of this big task force of 3000 plus soldiers, it was daunting to say the least. Our concept of getting this job done was to construct the ranges in phases and we name them Graf '82, Graf '83 and 84. Phase 82 required the upgrade or modernization of six ranges and phase 83 would have a requirement to upgrade four ranges. This concept of phasing allowed us to build the ranges in such a way as to handle a particular type of fighting vehicle and training cycle.

We mobilized to the Graf. training site so as to begin work on April 1, of each year and our schedule call for us to be complete in December of that same year. Phase three would be the final phase and was scheduled to be completed in December 1984. The phasing was linked to a year and was obviously necessary to minimize the impact on training and readiness for this critical equipment. The entire cost estimate at that time was roughly $82 million. The big savings on total cost was the use of the 18th Engineer Brigade and the other construction engineer capability in the command rather than a private contractor. The labor alone was a big savings to the command and it made good business sense to go this route for this type project when funds were scarce.

The scope of work for the Brigade was a responsibility for construction of the staging compound and all vertical and horizontal tasks down range. The commercial scope of work was obviously much smaller and consisted of electrical, emplacement of moving targets systems, and water well construction. This opportunity to construct this range upgrade project offered the best training the Brigade could expect as it required a full mobilization and demobilization effort. It also provided a platform that was close to war-like conditions and was a little tough on the families from the five communities around the command. The project was labeled as the largest troop construction project since World War II and I totally concurred with that assessment. The Brigade worked non-stop with its 3700 soldiers and hundreds of pieces of equipment during the construction season.

Staff Meeting at Graf.

This was without question the best training engineer's soldiers could get or hope for in peace time. After the first phase of the project was completed the soldiers who participated on the project were the best trained soldiers I had seen in 20 years. At the time of the project, there was a lot being said about the quality of our soldiers and specifically how they would hold up under stressful work situations. Having led these 3700 soldiers in a difficult wartime like environment, there was no doubt in my mind that they could hold up in a real war setting.

The working conditions were not always favorable and the worst part was putting up with the changing weather. The rain, mud, and all caused big problem for us. A good rain could delay us for two to three days and as a result we had to take care of the water from the rain and then repair any damage that was done as soon as possible. At times, it seems as if we were spending more time putting in temporary drainage work than anything else. We made over a 100 field changes during the first year and our soldiers learned a lot about how to do a big project.

In much the same way, we had great concern about morale and keeping the soldiers production at a level to ensure schedules and timelines were met. The number one concern was to ensure that the families that were left for 8-9 months back in the communities were okay. To that end, we briefed the families on the project, put in place good communication arrangements and organized the wives group into support cells. These arrangements worked very well and the concern for time away by the sponsors was mitigated by the care and concern displayed throughout those communities. My wife and the other wives in the Brigade led this effort and made it work every well. I am so proud of her work and leadership on this front.

We leased large air conditioned buses to transport some sponsors home on the weekends and also used these same buses to take families from the communities down to the training construction site on special event days. This transportation arrangement worked well for us and went a long way to keep morale in line. The family days were outstanding events and as a result, the Brigade would shut down work and allow the soldiers to spend maximum time with families. The activities for the children and adults were well organized and loaded with fun, food and excitement for all.

Another morale builder was our weekly Brigade two mile early morning run. This was an activity where every able soldier in the Brigade task force would participate in the two mile run early in the morning. This was great fun to be a part of and a real sight to see 3000+ soldiers going through the road network of the training complex. We often invited the senior commanders and others' on post or visiting to participate and to observe this training activity. We timed this event prior to breakfast and normal work hours and it was always successful.

Our soldiers were tightly knitted together during this period and had a lot of pride in what they were doing for the readiness of the Army in general, especially in Europe. As a result, we had no major discipline issues and maintained one of the best re-enlistment and accident records in the theater. The production requirements for the Brigade were high and performance was a high. This was a job requirement set for training that under normal circumstance would have been executed entirely by a commercial construction firm. It provided the best training (short of war) that could be had, and each soldier knew that. Our spot awards and on-site ceremonies were great boosters for morale as well. We found ways to pause and recognize our soldiers at every opportunity. It should be noted that our German Labor service organization (Battalion Size) was also with us on this task. This organization was very experienced in construction (particularly vertical construction) and played a significant role in the brigade's success with this project. We included this organization in all that we did as a brigade and the bond between them and us was strong. We were one team, one organization with the same mission.

Each of my U.S. battalions was unique in personality. The 293rd Engineer Battalion was a hard charging "do it right the first time" organization. It took on some of our toughest work. LTC Jude Paton was its commander in Graf '82 and LTC John Horne was commander in Graf '83/'84 and they knew how to get results. The 97th Engineer Battalion was very skilled in heavy construction. They were low key and did superb work on all jobs. LTC Doug Church was its commander in Graf '82 and LTC Milt Hunter was commander in Graf '83/'84. The 249th Engineer Battalion was a busy organization that was always ready to take on more. LTC Dale Means was its commander in Graf '82. LTC Peter Cahill was commander in Graf '83/'84. As was with the others, it got the job done and was effective. The 94th Engineer Battalion was also a very methodical organization that produced great quality. LTC Tom Geoffrey was the commander. The 649th TOPO Battalion handled our surveying and topographic task and did it well. The Battalion commanded by LTC Ken Kessler was well disciplined and enjoyed being among the heavy construction works. We were augmented from two Corps with, the 237th Engineer Battalion, the 317th Engineer Battalion, the 54th Engineer Battalion, the 82nd Engineer Battalion, the 547th Engineer Battalion and 16th Engineer Battalion. In fact, all of the battalion commanders who worked for me on the project got promoted at least one grade higher and LTC Ballard, Patin, Monroe and Hunter were promoted to General Officers. I was fortunate to have some of the best engineer Lieutenant Colonels in our Corps and the Army on this job. The brigade kept the project on schedule and delivered modernized and workable ranges as required. It was a very tough assignment but the attitude of the soldiers and officers was absolutely phenomenal.

My Commanders at Graf -1983.

Enough cannot be said about the families that were left back in the communities. It was not easy for them to manage without the sponsor being there to help. As stated earlier in this chapter, this range modernization project had all the trimmings of war (except the actual flight) and there was an impact on the families. We tried to anticipate the rough spots and made many provisions to counteract any concerns. My wife and the rest of the ladies really worked hard to keep morale and activities up and provided assistance in so many areas. As we began to work through the second year, there was a little push back from a few families on the long periods (8 months) of absence. Again, I cannot say enough about how well the wives work to keep the lid on each community. I would talk to my wife each day when I was at the training site to stay abreast of what was going on and she was a good sounding board for me on all of the community activities, including the host country concerns. Our construction activities were split between Graf training site and Wildflecken training area. This split operation generated coordination and communication challenges for us. We knew this split arrangement was in the cards, so our plans were to prepare to accommodate this structure. Again, I cannot say enough for the attitude, discipline and work ethic of the officers and enlisted men and women who took this ride with us. They were terrific!

On the host country front, I was able to keep the partnerships that had been established between our brigade and other German and French units back in the communities, in fact during this training. We found a way to include them in tours and other activities even when we were away at Graf. These arrangements worked very well for us across the board.

Every administrative and operational activity that would have been done back in our home communities continued while at the Graf training site. As an example, re-enlistments and retirements were examples of two such activities that were center to our many ceremonies. The opportunity to do this range modernization project was truly a shot in the arm for all of construction engineer soldiers. It even was a plus for all the support personnel as well. We had a battalion size organization supporting us in maintenance and they too did a superb job.

Thanking the soldiers for a job well done.

We tried to balance the long hours and hard work with officer's calls and "dining ins" for the officers and senior non-commissioned officers and other relaxing type events for the rest of the soldiers. This helped the leadership frame an environment that built cohesion and a caring command climate. The delicate work on these ranges was to lash up the command work with the troop construction. As mentioned the horizontal and vertical construction up and down range was accomplished by the brigade, and the moving targets and etc. installation was the responsibility the command sector with a private contractor. The quality control of this connectivity was delicate and was done very well. The commercial firms were all complimentary of the Brigade's work.

The number of senior visitors to the site was high and they ranged from the USAREUR Commander Gen. Kroesen, the Deputy Commander of USAREUR, each Corps Commander came, and many other senior leaders of the command and from the states. LTG Becton made a special visit during his trip to Europe as the Chief of training for the Training and Doctrine Command. He had promised that he would visit the project a year earlier when he attended my change of Command ceremony. It meant a lot to me and the Brigade for him to visit the site in his new capacity.

The construction duration each year was approximately eight months. This schedule caused the Brigade to mobilize to the site in late March and demobilize in early December. From a morale stand point, this allowed the soldiers to be home with families for the holidays in December and January. The close out of the site was a methodical process as everything had to be taken down and brought back to the respective communities. This included all equipment, soldier support supplies and some materials. Once the equipment was cleaned, inventoried and load on trains for transport to the home communities, the close out ceremony at the training site was the final major activity. This close out event involved the commander-in-Chief of USAREUR (General Frederick Kroesen) and this was a treat for the entire task force. The ceremony included awards and recognition coupled with a full dress parade and inspection in ranks by the commander, a very colorful ceremony that allowed the senior leader to officially thank and express his appreciation for 8 months of hard work and super training. Gen. Kroesen always found time to spare time on his calendar for this event, and it was appreciated by all the soldiers.

My Big Boss, Commander-in-Chief of USAREUR, General Frederick Kroesen.

Upon arriving back into our respective communities, it was back to work with unloading of equipment and getting it settle in for maintenance during the winter months. This was followed by leaves and vacations with families and friends. It was amazing to witness the strong bond between the soldiers and the high morale that stayed in place after returning to the home communities. The media was all over this unique project and the most important aspect was to capture the training value. I gave many presentations and was interviewed over and over by the press on the project. It was truly the largest troop construction project since World War II and clearly one-of-a kind.

Going Home.

German/American Relations

One of the most challenging and delicate responsibilities as community commander was the maintenance of healthy German/American relationship. I met and got to know very well those local, state and some Federal level officials early on in my command tour. There were challenges that require a delicate touch by both sides and these good working relationships were vital. One situation of particular significance was the access/visits by our soldiers to the local entertainment/facilities and bars in the city of Karlsruhe. The issue created morale problem for the command and few law enforcement issues for the local officials. Our solution (suggested by me) was to have the Chief of Police, Mayor of Karlsruhe and myself to visit all sixteen bars in question on a designated evening to see the situation first hand. The three of us met at a pre-defined location and went out for the visits which consumed all the evening and until sometime after midnight. We visited each bar, talk to many people who were visiting the bar and had long conversations with the bar/club owners. This approach was a huge success and the owners all met a few days after our visit and agreed to allow all American soldiers to visit those establishments starting with the following weekend. The local newspapers and our U.S. paper *Stars and Stripes* gave great coverage on this matter as it was a major breakthrough for improving German/American relations.

The previous Attorney General was assassinated at this site.

As a result of this breakthrough and my on-going military partnership with a German unit led by Col. Langkop, the German/American relations in our community became a model. Langkop was a strong commander who really believed in good German/American relationship and went the extra mile to make team work. A significant example of his strong feelings about our unit's relationship was when he arranged and invited me to plant a tree on the property that housed his unit. It was a prominent location in Karlsruhe and the tree has a brass plate carrying my name.

Command of Brigade

The German American relations were key to successful command in Germany at this time. It was important to have a partnership with a German military organization. VVK 52 commanded by Col. Gunter Langkop who was my partnership unit. We trained together, socialized together and most of all worked as a team on host nation issues. We participated in many field exercises and the one which comes to mind as being significant was exercise "wintex" where we accomplished a joint mission very successfully. Col. Langkop played a pivotal role in the recommendation for me to be awarded the large German Cross award. This was the most prestigious peacetime award given by the German government. It was also the first award of its kind given to an African American commander. It was a distinct honor.

Receiving the "Large German Cross" (Großes Verdienstkreuz).

German Major General Butler offers congratulations.

The unique interaction that was laced with mutual respect was another major "sign post" along my road. The bottom line was this relationship played a key role in me having a very successful command tour. The Karlsruhe military community and the 18th Engineer Brigade were truly better organizations with superb German American relations when I departed.

On the Federal side, the Attorney General of the Federal Republic of Germany (Herr Redmon) visited our government house for a reception and I did the same at his home in Stuttgart for receptions and dinners. The local Mayor and all the senior leaders located in Karlsruhe, our other good and close friends along with military representation from the whole community attended the reception for the Attorney General. It did help that I could speak some of the German language and understood most of it from my training at the language school prior to this assignment.

Thinking it over.

As recognition of this unique relationship, the President of the Federal Republic of Germany (equivalent of our President of the United States) approved the award of the Large German Cross for me a few months prior to my departure. I might add this was the highest award/medal that could be bestowed on a foreign official by the German Government for service at that time. I was grateful for the award which was presented to me by Major General Butler, the German General in my sector. It was an honor for General Butler to do this on behalf of the President of the Federal Republic, and he was also friend and partner.

My wife maintained excellent contact and participated in many of the wives activities sponsored by the German ladies (i.e. cooking and bridge clubs). A delegation of twenty of these ladies came to the United States for a vacation and made a special trip to New York on Governors Island to visit with us after our tour was over. This was a real testament of the strength of this relationship. It was one of the best that I have witnessed and I view this experience as a major sign post on "My Road."

Selection to Brigadier General

I was fortunate to be selected for promotion to Brigadier General at the end of my second year in command. This was good news for my family and me but equally great news for the military community (including the local nationals) and the Brigade. This selection for General Officer was a major step forward and was a testament to much hard work and a positive indication that I had moved from that dirt road in Alabama and was now heading for the super highway. As I stood in the beautiful SLOSS garden in Karlsruhe waiting to be promoted to Brigadier General Officer, I had a quick reflection as we stood on the beautiful lawn of the SLOSS garden in Karlsruhe Germany and realized that it was how my great grandmother had said, "everything was really going to be all right." It was not easy to say good bye to so many friends, the soldiers and families. We left immediately after the ceremony was over with both happy and sad feelings and yes, some tears. I could still imagine her whisper ringing in my ear… The voice of my great-grandmother saying, "I knew you could do it my boy."

Promotion to General Officer (The penning of the Star by my wife and LTG Ayers).

Handshake after the promotion to Brigadier General (BG).

Patty at University of Virginia (UVA)

Patty, our oldest child started at the University of Virginia a year prior to us departing to Germany for command. It was a tough decision to leave her here while the entire family went off to Europe but those were the cards we were dealt. We purchased her a car and made certain that she could visit with her grandparents in North Carolina. It was tough on all of us but she made it through the required four years. She came to Germany during all the school breaks except Thanksgiving and my wife would make one trip back to visit her on campus each year. After graduation, Patty came to Germany and joined us for our last year. She landed a job with the American Express Company and did quite a bit of traveling. We were very proud of her. She is now a very successful school teacher, married and she and her husband, William, have two children (Alicia and Alex).

Chuck, Jr. at West Point (USMA)

Chuck received a Presidential appointment and entered the military academy at West Point after spending his senior year in Germany. All went well with his education and training over the four years. He participated in sports and was one of the top senior leaders of his class. He decided not become an engineer but rather an economist and selected Armor as a branch of service. We all attended his graduation ceremony and Marge and I had the pleasure of pinning on his Second

Lieutenant bars during the activities. (I used my Second Lieutenant bars for this occasion.) Chuck, Jr. has done well in his career and retired with the rank of Colonel, and he has two children (Chuck III and Christina).

Calvin at Virginia Military Institute (VMI)

Our youngest child entered Virginia Military Institute as we traveled home from our assignment in Germany. He had a very tough schedule at VMI – playing varsity football, majoring in Civil Engineering and dealing with all the rest of that came with this all-male institute program. As with the other two children, he did well and graduated with his degree in Civil Engineering. He wanted to go to work as a young Engineer right away – and he did in Georgia. This was followed with jobs in Louisiana and Mississippi. He got a big dose of the southern living early on in his career and enjoyed it all. He learned fast, did very well and is a solid Civil Engineer and senior project manager. Calvin has two children (Calvin II and Collin).

My Wife's Reflections On "My Road"

It has always been a pleasure for me to talk about my husband. In the military, we wives do that all day.

Chuck is very private. Everything he does is by a schedule and in order.

Many people and even I have asked him, "Why don't you write a book?" The important fact is Chuck has put his pen on paper and wrote his life's story titled "My Road." With God as his rock, Chuck has been rewarded with a wonderful family that was waiting for him at home. I have proudly shared his road with him for over fifty years. There have been some deep valleys and rocky paths, but with God's help we always managed to stay on the right road. He never wanted me to work away from home. At the beginning of our marriage, my life was centered around the children and Chuck's work. I enjoyed attending teas and coffees in the morning or afternoon with the other military spouses. My joy was playing bridge with the ladies' club. I was always a winner. When our first child, Patty was born, I would play bridge with her on my lap. I was always at home to prepare for dinner for Chuck where we would sit down for dinner and he would tell me about the events of his day at work from the beginning to the end. It was always interesting. He enjoyed his dinner at home especially looking forward to my desserts. I really enjoyed that part of the day because I had a chance to tell him of my experiences of the day and he enjoyed listening to me talk about my day with the ladies also.

On Sundays, we were in church or Chapel with our family. We tried to attend church every Sunday because a strong background of faith was always an important foundation. Our friends often said to us when you see one, you would always know the other is not far behind. We have always been inseparable. The only time we have been really separated during our marriage is when Chuck was in Vietnam. Even then, we found a way to meet in Hawaii during Chuck's R&R breaks.

We moved quite frequently while in the military, about every three years. In spite of this, I did pursue my teaching profession when Chuck was in Vietnam, during his graduate school, or stationed in the Washington, DC area and New York City. This was something I wanted to do. It was a joy to see how well we did keeping up with the children and to have children who embraced and still enjoying the Army life just as much as we have.

In the Washington, DC area, the children were involved in little league activity. Chuck decided he would coach the boys in little league football and basketball. Chuck would carry with him on each practice day a change of clothes and I would meet him at the field with the boys. Meanwhile, I would drive our daughter to her dance lessons and she joined the Cheerleaders at her high school. We would all arrive home about the same time. The boys played little league football and basketball until Middle School then they joined the school's sports program and became top athletes.

Our daughter, Patty graduated from High School and the family took a trip to Saint Thomas, Virgin Islands to celebrate. When we arrived home, Chuck was on the list to the Army War College and also about a month later he was on the Colonel's promotion list. Chuck's road was moving on the fast track and he was also. We knew that after the War College his road would lead him back to Washington area and then overseas. This would give us a year to be here with Patty and see her through the first year of college before we left the area for Germany.

It was hard for me to leave our daughter here, and this was one part of his road that had a valley. Chuck walked his road with pride. I was left here to get our daughter back in school and to wait until the boys had completed the year. Our daughter would visit my parents in North Carolina when she was out of college for short breaks. The boys, Skippy and I arrived in Germany with a great welcome from hubby and several friendly faces. Chuck was faced with the opportunity to have his road expanding even longer and wider. I was confident that he would do well. Chuck had a big responsibility as American Mayor of Karlsruhe and Commander of the 18th Engineer Brigade. Living in Germany again was quite enjoyable and different from our first tour there. Chuck's road was getting longer and with many curves. We would talk and laugh every night about how wonderful it was to have developed so many German friends. At one period he was away for almost four days a week but he walked his road with pride and control because he straighten every curve along the way. He was the best Commander Karlsruhe ever had. Christmas was very special for us because the family was always together and we really enjoyed traveling together. We returned to Virginia and we were excited to be home with family and friends. It was interesting to see how straight his path was going after making General. Both families were very proud. Chuck had started on his super highway and that led him to his second "Star."

This is my reflection on his life.

Marjorie Seymore Williams

Photo Section

Career and Family Highlights

Promotion to Captain.

Parent's weekend at West Point.

Two of Patty's professors congratulate her following her graduation from the University of Virginia.

Our daughter Patty's wedding day with her brothers Chuck and Calvin.

A leader throughout the experience, very proudly Chuck Williams, our son, receives congratulations during his graduation ceremony at West Point.

Below: Mother and Dad following the graduation at West Point.

At West Point following the pinning of our son Chuck Jr. with his 2nd Lt. rank. I used my old 2nd Lt bars for this historic occasion.

Our son Calvin graduating from Virginia Military Institute (VMI) with a BS degree in Civil Engineering and played varsity football.

Calvin Edmond Williams

CW, C, Rif
Army — Civil Engineering
Alexandria, Virginia

Above: Marjorie and the kids at a Richmond, VA amusement park.

The Williams' at home in our Governor's Island quarters.

Marjorie's parents celebrate their 50th wedding anniversary. Pictured are family members at this blessed event.

Our military home on Governor's Island, NY.

At home, Sunday moring before church.

After church services.

Our first military ball after assuming brigade command in Germany.

Family photo while attending the Army's Command and General Staff College leadership training.

Daughter Patty and my wife Marjorie visiting my office at the State Department for a lunch date.

LT General Becton, a mentor, visiting me at Graf.

LTG John Forrest, my immediate boss with me at Graf.

Above: The prestigious Excellence Award presented to the 18th Engineer Brigade.

General Otis, my big boss observing the new ranges in Germany.

The brigade change of command in Germany.

Our good German friends, Colonel and Mrs. Manfred Wolfe.

Above: Mrs. Williams being escorted to her seat at my promotion to Brigadier General ceremony.

Right: Reviewing the troops after the promotion ceremony with COL Miles.

Promotion Ceremony to Brigadier General (my wife assisting with the penning)

Below: Standing Tall after being promoted to General.

FINAL SALUTE AFTER PROMOTION TO BRIGADIER GENERAL

Following the reception after our change of command in New York City.

Below: A Presidential Citation from the Comander in Chief, President George Bush.

CERTIFICATE OF APPRECIATION

FOR SERVICE IN THE ARMED FORCES OF THE UNITED STATES

Major General Charles E. Williams
United States Army

I extend to you my personal thanks and the sincere appreciation of a grateful nation for your contribution of honorable service to our country. You have helped maintain the security of the nation during a critical time in its history with a devotion to duty and a spirit of sacrifice in keeping with the proud tradition of the military service.

I trust that in the coming years you will maintain an active interest in the Armed Forces and the purposes for which you served.

My best wishes to you for happiness and success in the future.

George Bush

COMMANDER IN CHIEF

Constructor magazine cover featured me and highlighted my accomplishments in the global construction marketplace in a feature story.

Alicia, our oldest granddaughter, a Magna Cum Laude graduate from our alma mater the renowned Tuskegee University, where I serve as Chairman of the Board of Trustees.

The family attends Alicia's graduation at Tuskegee University.

Williams Family Heritage

My Great Grandmother, Annie Long Ellis affectionately known as "Bannie."

My father,
Roosevelt Williams

My mother,
Mattie Wallace Williams

Granddad and Grandmother,
Robert and Emma Williams

The Williams family reunion in Alabama.

The Williams brothers at a wedding.

My brothers and sisters at one our annual reunuions (I am 3rd from the left).

The Williams family reunion in Alabama.

The grandchildren: *(left to right)* Alex, Alicia, Chuck III, Calvin II, Collin, and Christina.

Grandchildren and children celebrating our 50th Wedding Anniversary in Kitty Hawk, NC.

Flowers for my wife following my promotion ceremony to Major General.

Marjorie assisting in the penning of my 2nd star.

LT Gen Max and Priscilla Noah visiting us at Governor's Island for our Command Dining-in.

The new Major General and Mrs. Williams.

At a State Department function.

A church event as Chairman of the Board of Trustees, the board is concluding the largest loan for renovation in the church's history.

After the swearing in as the first Director/COO of the new Overseas Buildings Operations - in Secretary Powell's office.

Happy days at the State Department. A pure joy to work together.

Secretary Powell visits the office of Overseas Buildings Operation.

With our good friend, Mrs. Alma Powell, wife of U.S. Secretary of State Colin Powell.

THE CONSTRUCTION WEEKLY
May 23, 2005 • enr.com
The McGraw-Hill Companies

ENR
Engineering News-Record

Closing
Military base reductions produce promise, pain

Cleaning Up
EPA rule will cost utilities $15 billion to cap emissions

Flat
Shortage of radial tires crimps equipment owners

Opening Performance

Discipline and accountability set stage for success of U.S. embassy program

Charles E. Williams
Director/Chief Operating Officer
Overseas Buildings Operations
U.S. Dept. of State

McGraw_Hill CONSTRUCTION

News maker - ENR magazine highlights my accomplishments as U.S. Dept. of State Director of Overseas Building Operations and the building of 50 new U.S. Embassies.

Secretary Powell, Deputy Secretary Armitage, Mrs. Powell and my wife with me at a State Department Activity.

Secretary Powell visits the OBO staff meeting.

Visiting Tiananmen Square in Beijing, China.

Above: Sightseeing at the Great Wall of China.

Below: Visiting the Rock of Gibraltar.

Top right: Standing with villiage Chiefs at the ground-breaking of the new embassy site in Cote d'Ivoire.

Bottom right: Marge, me, Ambassador Render and the Education Chief of Cote d'Ivioire

President Rochon and Board of Trustees Chairman Charles E. Williams present Board of Trustees Chair Emeritus Andrew F. Brimmer (center) with a Doctor of Laws degree.

General and Mrs. Charles E. Williams, a striking couple out for a special evening at Tuskegee University.

Seven

The Big Hills

As we started traveling the autobahn from Karlsruhe to Frankfurt (Rhine Main Airport) for our trip back to United States, I realized that this had been a historic three years in my life. It had been further punctuated by the Army and my country selecting the first African American General Officer from Army Corps of Engineers who had not attend the military academy and the second African General in the entire Army Corps of Engineers. At the same time I was reflecting on the notion of having received the Federal Republic of Germany's decoration of the Large German Cross which was the highest medal that the Federal Republic of Germany could give to an American for service and the facilitation of German and American relationships. The tears began to dry up and sadness of leaving this high performing organization, friends, and host country were no longer a problem for me to cope with. I knew the "storm was not over" but the road signs on My Road was pointing to the *super highway*—the Top.

The family was very quiet on the ride from Karlsruhe to Rhine Main Air Force Base. I knew that there were many good thoughts flowing through all of our heads. Some of these must have been:

- Our daughter had graduated from the University of Virginia a year prior and spent the last year with us in Germany.

- Our oldest son was in his second year at the Military Academy at West Point and was doing very well.

- Our youngest son was on his way to enter into Virginia Military Institute (VMI) as soon as we returned home.

- My wife was reflecting on how many true German friends she had made and her role as the Commander's wife in a very big and tough assignment.

- We were on our way home to a great assignment after a successful command tour.

- I was reflecting on the road I had traveled so far and where it would lead me in the future; that was big on my mind.

- How hard work could pay off and set the azimuth for the future when you push for excellence.

- Was now a General Officer at age 46 (24 years in the Army)

- Full knowledge that this could only happen to me in the United States of America.

- I was constantly reminded of the thought that such loyal and devoted soldiers played a key role in my success—I will never forget them.

Director of Operations and Maintenance Appropriations

This was my second Washington assignment at the Pentagon. It was a delightful experience to return back to the Pentagon and the Office of the Comptroller of the Army as the Director, Operations and Maintenance appropriations. Having served in this same directorate for several years prior as a Major and Lt. Colonel and now with the opportunity to return and serve as the Director could only happen in America. Since I was not new in this environment, and knew my way around the directorate and the Pentagon, I hit the ground running.

I had the opportunity to work for the then Comptroller of the Army, Lt. General Max Noah. Max was an analytical-grounded manager, with an electrical engineering degree and cadet nick name at West Point as "Juice." He dealt deep into the numbers and was very good at getting to the root of every issue. He and I lashed up very well because he pushed everyone toward excellence and constantly looked for new and improved methods and means to get the job done. Max was a good leader and did not micro manage me, but he watched the results that I produced very closely and that was a good thing for performance and accountability. We had a $21 billion Operations and Maintenance Appropriations Budget during the peak of this two year assignment and I believe we served our Army well in managing the appropriations. I recall traveling quite a bit around the Army to assess how our Operations and Maintenance dollars were being utilized and to garner first-hand knowledge from top officials as to what the funding needs would be in the future. I recall very interesting experiences during my travels to visit the field over this two year period.

The first was a visit to South Korea where we had some unique and delicate funding requirements. This visit took me to several sites in Korea, looking at base operations support requirements, the troops and training. The highlight of this particular trip was visiting the Korean peninsula border (Panmunjom), to witness our soldiers and North Korean guards standing tall, almost touching each other as they were protecting their countries turf. I was taken by this experience and spent some time talking to our soldiers about this command and the delicate mission. One cannot imagine this, but would have to see it first-hand to understand what the result from a war can have on us. On the trip back from Panmunjom, I began to reflect on what I had just experienced and a few questions came in my mind. They were:

1. Will the day ever come when we do not have borders or walls to divide a country?
2. Will the people from the same blood and some remote cases of the same family tree ever come together as one country?

With these unanswered questions, my premises once again validated that "this storm was not over" and there was still a reason and a requirement to keep pushing.

This was a very interesting "sign post" along *My Road* because it left a lasting impression.

The second experience during my tour of duty as the Director of Operations and Maintenance was a visit to the Military Academy at West Point. It goes without saying that this historical institution that produced Generals MacArthur, Patten, and Eisenhower has a unique place in our history. I had an opportunity as Director of Operations and Maintenance appropriation to be responsible for its funding. As stated earlier in this book; I was not a West Point graduate and was always somewhat curious as to what this institution was about. On this visit, I asked a lot of questions and visited most of the buildings, and even broke ground for a new commissary. Our son Chuck, Jr., was in his second year at the academy and it was after this trip that I began to feel like a graduate. It was truly an amazing educational institution for a lot of the preparation had to deal with the big issues. I was impressed!

As I approached the end of the second year in this job, I was fortunate to be selected as the Division Commander of the North Atlantic Division, U.S. Army Corps of Engineers with duty station in New York City. This Division command selection was strongly recommended and supported by Lieutenant General Elvin R. Heiberg III and my current boss, Lieutenant General Max Noah. This was a great command assignment for an engineer general since it was a Major General's billet and I was still a Brigadier General. The division had a very rich history and a string of top flight commanders before me.

The North Atlantic Division is currently one of eight U.S. Army Corps of Engineers regional business centers that efficiently and effectively deliver projects and services to the Armed Forces, the nation, and the international community. It includes six districts as well as the Belvoir Integration Office which oversees military programs at Fort Belvoir, Va. Through the Europe District, NAD also supports the US European and US Africa commands.

The division worked in the northeastern states, District of Columbia, Europe, and anywhere else in the world where it was needed. As an engineering and project management organization, we plan, design, build, operate and maintain projects to support the military, protect

America's water resources, and restore and enhance the environment. The work includes a variety of engineering and construction for international, federal, state, and local governments and agencies.

North Atlantic Division Commander

Like all the rest of my assignments, this move from Virginia to New York caused a revamping of some aspects of my family's lifestyle. This assignment required us to move to New York, and we were fortunate that a historic set of General Officer's quarters were on Governors Island, a Coast Guard base in New York City. There were many interesting and unique things about this housing location, but I will only illuminate a few. It required a ferry ride of 10 minutes or so from Lower Manhattan (Battery Park City) over to Governors Island. Most people walked from the ferry once it docked on Governors Island to wherever they were going. It was unique to live on this Coast Guard base and interesting to get to know senior counterparts of this service.

As stated, the command's boundaries encompassed a huge area and had a big support responsibility. This command, North Atlantic Division had only five districts at that time, spanning from Maine down through Virginia and was very busy with three very visible projects during my tenure. The first was re-planning and rebuilding of Ft. Drum located in up-state New York (I will come back to this one later because there is much to say about it). Second was the deepening of the channels in the ports to accommodate deep draft cargo vessels in New York/New Jersey, Philadelphia, Baltimore, and Norfolk. This channel deepening was very delicate because at each location we had a specific depth requirement that had to be met and it was expensive work. The third was to renovate/rebuild the south end of military academy at

West Point. This requirement called for a restoration of the Lady Cliff Women's College, which had been acquired by West Point and also adding some other major renovations to that end of campus. It goes without saying that this was delicate work that received more than its share of external oversight. The Division had an assortment of other projects down the east coast (both civil and military). We built and maintained jetties and inlets to assist with water traffic navigation; constructed installation facilities and did airport work; many water projects and other construction in each of the district sectors. The Division was very active in the region and participated in many community activities. It goes without saying that our military customers throughout the Division were special and our relationship was outstanding during this tour of duty.

Another significant event occurred at the beginning of this command assignment and it was the graduation of our oldest son from West Point. I recall this was a special occasion and all our family came to West Point to witness this "first" in our family. I was honored to share in the actual promoting of him to an Army Officer (Second Lieutenant). He had chosen Armor as his branch of service and was very excited about this choice. Both my father and my wife's father were very sick with cancer but they made arrangements and did make the trip to West Point to see their first grandson graduate from this historic institution. The days that we spent together during the graduation activities were so meaningful to them and the rest of the family.

We assembled at Governor's Island (where we lived) after the graduation to reflect and relax prior to the family members returning home. This was a "sign post" along *My Road* that I will always remember and cherish.

During this assignment, I met the individual who labeled himself as the Dean of the Corps of Engineers Officers in New York City. He was Col (Ret) Joe Markle. He truly had the Corps of Engineers at heart and soul and would make that known very forcefully to all (especially new commanders). He was loyal to the Corps and its principles and attended all Corps of Engineer activities in New York City. He was without question Mr. "Corps of Engineers" in New York City.

The then Chairman of the Joint Chief of Staff, Gen. Colin Powell came to New York to speak and also was very interested in how Ft. Drum was coming along.

Regional VP of Society American Military Engineers

The annual Engineer activities that were set each year around the first weekend of November was always a delight. Everyone tried to attend (retired and active) and Col. Markle was always center stage with the arrangement and etc. It was a great opportunity to relax and mingle with the Corps of Engineer leaders. I also served as the Regional Vice President of the Society of American Engineers (SAME). Our focus was on the mentoring and the development of students who were interested in the profession.

My selection and appointment as Regional Vice President of the New York – New Jersey areas of the Society of American Engineers was almost as historical as my being the first African American to command the North Atlantic Division. This appointment had "juice" and ranked high on the list because of the people it represented (i.e. most of New York, New Jersey and the mid-Atlantic states). The United States

Military Academy was in this footprint and all of this made it a unique experience. I recall that cold evening in November at our regional command black tie SAME event when I was designated and accepted the appointment as Regional VP. This event took place at the Waldorf Astoria Hotel in New York City. My Society of American Military Engineer (SAME) responsibilities took me to the campus of West Point and throughout New Jersey participating in student posts activities. This appointment also kept me very close to Col (Ret) Joe Markel as well.

Going to the podium at the Society of American Military Engineers' event at the Waldorf Astoria Hotel in New York.

LTG Heiberg and members of the Society of American Military Engineers pictured with my wife and me at the Waldorf Astoria Hotel event.

This was truly quite an evening with a packed house. As I left my seat and started to walk toward the podium to accept the appointment, I could not help from reflecting on *"My Road"* for and where it has taken me so far. I thought for a quick moment of where *My Road* started and also on my current responsibilities:

- Managing the rebuilding of a major Army installation (Ft. Drum - $1.3 B)

- Managing the rebuilding/renovation of the south end of the West Point Military Academy Campus (including the campus of Ladycliff College)

- Managing the Channel Deepening project of our major ports along the east coast (New York – New Jersey, Philadelphia, Baltimore and Norfolk)

These were big historic projects that offered unique opportunities to manage. I thought also about what a wonderful time to serve and manage something big in my country and said to myself, "Only in America."

Re-building of Ft. Drum

The Ft. Drum project was big, visible and different. It was "fast paced" and expensive. It was unique in that it was the rebuilding of existing base that had been around since WWII. Its new configuration was designed such that it could accommodate our new light infantry structure. This installation was located about 100 miles south of the Canadian border and in the frigid temperature area of upstate New York. I recall the town of Watertown was very patriotic and supportive of military activity at this installation and the region. For that reason, this new facility was well accepted by the local environment. The temperature in the winter was very cold, reported average snowfall was 23 inches and it made construction very difficult during the winter months. The project was planned differently and funded different from the rest of the military construction budget. I recall there may have been three different types of funding associated with this project that generated more than $500 million for a single contract. I believe this was recorded at that time as the largest single contract that had been let for a troop facility.

In addition to a reconstructed airfield and many buildings including Brigade and Battalion complexes, Commissary, PX, recreation, and etc., it had several hundred sets of family housing on post and thousand more to be built off post. It was a massive project that had to be completed within record time. One of the critical pacing items for this project was the construction of the housing. It goes without saying that the need for housing, soldiers and families were critical for rapid establishing of the new base structure. After the contract was let for the major construction, it progressed along a tight schedule, pretty much as planned. I recall that there were miles and miles of infrastructure, piping, cabling, etc. and the erection of overhead a water tower that would be the signature of the new Ft. Drum complex.

Assistant Secretary of the Army (AWASA-CW) visits Ft. Drum.

The housing construction task was another story, in that, the majority of the housing had to be in the neighboring community around the base. The acquisition concept used for this housing was the section 801. This housing initiative allowed the private sector firms to acquire property to build on, and then build housing to the Army's specification and schedule. The Army would then guarantee the builder a certain level of occupancy for each housing section and the Army would draw from the service members housing allowance to satisfy the lease. This private-type arrangement was a new concept for many but worked quite well for rapid building of housing development around Ft. Drum. I made many visit to Ft. Drum to observe this 2800 unit housing project while it was under construction and was impressed with the new "fast track" approach. I was also pleased with quality, the layout of each community, proximity to the base, and the basic design for each community. In fact, the builders literally tried very hard to outperform each other. This was a smart concept for our Army to rapidly acquire housing for a new organization.

There were many other types of facilities that were a part of this effort. Some of these were social clubs, a guest house, child care center, fire station and etc. This new post construction drew the similar visitors from the Army and also foreign officials as well. As we were building the new installation, the 10th mountain division (light infantry) was training rapidly to stand up as quickly as possible. All of this made a very crowded post with not much room to spare during the height of construction. This installation near Watertown, N.Y. is a good location for a military installation in that strong local support was in place. I learned of my selection for Major General while on one of my regular visits to Ft. Drum. This dual function of managing the Division that was one of the busiest in the Corps at that time really taxed me. I recall having other active projects as far north as Greenland and far south as the Dismal Swamp in Chesapeake Virginia. It was tough on my wife since I was gone three days in every week to Ft. Drum, but she managed very well on the Coast Guard base of Governors Island in New York City.

Moving toward the Results-Based Organization Concept

This project was very large and highly visible throughout the Army. We put in place a very tight and experienced on-site supervision team. This team was hand-picked and was loaded with the right skill sets to manage this fast track project. The accountability and performance against each type of funding was critical and required strong on-site management from start to finish.

The scope of work for this rebuilding of the installation included a host of office buildings, support buildings, infrastructure, utilities, recreation facilities, and an airfield upgrade. I recall the road network to be a critical task early on coupled with the cogeneration plant which provided both heat and high temperature hot water. This cogeneration plant was also a privatization project as well which required a contractor owned and operated arrangement. We were able to keep the tasks on schedule and the massive new military town begins to come out of the ground and take shape. I was traveling to and from New York City each week and usually stayed for two days to attend meetings, have program reviews and visit the construction.

The contractors were a large joint venture (Blackwater Contractors) that was capable of working seven days each week if necessary. Our first winter was a rough one as it produced several big snows and kept the temperature at the freezing level most of the time. Since the weather was generally bad during the winter in the constructed environment, we had covers for each building site, kept the temperature at a level that would allow the concrete to cure correctly. By any measure, this was an amazing project and the lessons learned from this project served all of us well going forward.

I was selected for promotion to Major General and a reassignment back to the Pentagon as Director of Management. This action cut my command tour short, but I was not about to turn down an opportunity to continue to serve my country in a very key capacity. It was packing time again and I was heading back to Washington, D.C. for the new assignment on the Army staff. This assignment would mark the fourth time during the past twelve years that I had been assigned to the Army staff at the Pentagon. There was no question that I knew my way around and all this helped with the transition into the new job. At this junction in my military career, My Road was very smooth and without bumps and there were no sharp curves. In summary, I was getting to the smooth riding super highway.

My promotion to Major General was done in a delightful ceremony in New York City. LTG Hank Hatch officiated the promotion in his capacity as the Chief of Engineers and my boss. My wife, Marge, was delighted to participate in the pining of my second star. The location was not too far from the Division Headquarters in Manhattan. It was another career milestone and another key sign post on My Road. It was unique in that along with the promotion there were orders to return back to Washington (the Pentagon) to serve as the Director of Management. It was difficult leaving the division and all the good friends we have made in New York City but that was what had to be done at that time.

One of our sons (Calvin) and our daughter (Patty and husband, William) were in attendance a long list of special friends along with a big representation from the division. This was a time for mixed feelings about leaving the division at a peak period for the opportunity to serve in one of the high visibility two star jobs in the Pentagon. Our project at Fort Drum was on schedule and in good shape, the Channels Deepening projects were almost finished and the rest of the division's tasks were under control. We had accomplished much during the two and a half years and our clients were pleased. This is one aspect of the military that is good where you leave with a feeling of a job well done. It gives one the opportunity to serve in a variety of jobs and when it is determined that your services are needed elsewhere, you must move on. This move back to Washington for my fourth assignment in the Pentagon would record our thirteenth move during our career.

Back to Washington – Pentagon, Director of Management

In this job, I worked directly for the Director of the Army Staff and sat in for him when he was away. I was in a position to get a good dose of the everyday challenges and issues of the Army and at the senior level. It was an exciting job in all aspects and my office was very close to the Generals Officers Mess (dining facility) and that was a plus around Noon every day. It was a big directorate with five-six divisions to supervise. One of these divisions was responsible for all the information management and big inventory of computers and related equipment that supported our Army staff requirements.

I recall LTG Mick Kicklighter being the Director of the Army Staff and a very good man. He was always curious about how we were doing our mission but never micro-managed. He and I became very good friends and worked well together. I recall him being very interested in how the Army's fleets of military aircraft were managed in support of the senior members of the Army. Another very exciting responsibility of the office was the management and oversight for Army's "Communities of Excellence" initiative. This was a program that was designed to improve the living and working conditions on all our post in the United States. It was focused on the community type improvements that impact morale of the soldiers and families. There was much competition and a big award for the winners each year. I had several full -time staff assigned to this program to ensure that the criteria for excellence was in play and followed. I traveled throughout the Army to gauge the program's progress and to see firsthand how it was being implemented. It was one of the Army's best programs for getting everyone involved in post improvements.

The other noteworthy responsibility that was very interesting was the opportunity served as the Army's point of contact for the first Defense Base Closure and Realignment action. This was a big task for the Army and it was laced with much emotion and very rigid positions. The effort was DOD led with the Army represented by its management office. I recall how difficult it was for the Army to come to a decision on the criteria and etc. for closure or realignment. I was aided by the fresh experience of building a new installation, Ft. Drum in upstate New York. Since this job requires essentially building for a new population and closing down the old, there was some similarity in this work.

I met frequently with my Navy and Air Force counterparts to coordinate on those cost-cutting issues. It was very tough and delicate work to build the case for or against and have the recommendations hold. We gave countless briefings to the Army staff seniors and maintained a very large database. This work required many late evenings and some weekends to meet the tight deadlines. The training and experience gained from this big visible task was unmeasured and served me well from the standpoint of understanding closures and realignment in the U.S. Army. It was in this job that I began to think about returning and moving on to the civilian world. There were two driving factors: (1) I was only 50 years old and in very good health, (2) I was receiving many opportunities to move to the private sector and I decided that it was time to retire. I was often asked by the seniors, "What motivated me to make the move to retire?" To that question, I saw two distinct reasons for me to leave: 1) I had an opportunity to continue to help with the public good (working for the children) by taking a responsibility that would improve the quality of the public school facilities in one of our largest cities; 2) I had done a lot for the U.S. Army and the Corps of Engineers over a span of twenty nine years ... and wanted to try civilian life. I can say today that it was truly the right decision and I did not look back and never regretted the decision. I accepted the job as President and CEO of the New York City's School Construction Authority. I was the first President/CEO as this was a new public authority set in place by the state legislature to address chronic public school maintenance and rebuilding problems. It goes without saying that this was not a popular action for the existing staff, but in my view it was the right one at that time. This school system had over one million students and was housed in a physical plant that had over 700 schools. A massive school system to say the least and "My Road" continued and was approaching the "fast lanes" of the super highway with this job.

EDUCATION

Major General Williams Heads Nation's Largest School Construction Authority

By GEORGE WOODS, JR.

Charles E. Williams, a highly-decorated former U.S. Army Major General who once managed the Army's $21 billion operations and maintenance appropriations and, while stationed in Germany, guided the Army's largest peacetime construction project since World War II is the President and Chief Executive Officer of New York City School Construction Authority.

A first-of-its-kind public benefit corporation created by the New York State Legislature in December 1988, Williams, a highly experienced executive manager, was selected to head the School Construction Authority.

As President, he is responsible for directing the Authority's program to design, build and rebuild New York City's deteriorating school buildings. The $4.3 billion budget makes it the largest school building program in the nation.

Earlier this month, The Authority broke ground on a $3.5 million extension to PS 169 in Brooklyn, one of the first of 30 such additions to be built around the city during the next five years.

After 29-year military career in which he supervised more than $6 billion worth of construction projects worldwide, he came to the Authority August 15, 1989. Prior to assuming this position, General Williams was Director of Management in the Office of the Army's Chief of Staff. He began his military career as a Second Lieutenant in 1960 in the Corp of Engineers.

For the next ten years he served in various command and staff assignments in the United States and overseas. Following a decade of assignments as management analyst, budget analyst and planner, he in 1981 was appointed commander of the 18th Engineer Brigade and the Karlsruhe Military Community in Germany. In addition to commanding this largest construction engineering unit in the Army, he served in a dual role as the U.S. Mayor of all American forces in his district.

From 1986-88, he was Commander of the North Atlantic Division of the Army Corps of Engineers with duty station in New York City. While in this position, he directed the planning, design and construction throughout 13 northwestern states.

His medals include: the Distinguished Service Medal (with Oak Leaf Cluster) the Legion of Merit (with two Oak Leaf Clusters); the Distinguished Flying Cross; the Bronze Star Medal (with Oak Leaf Cluster); the Federal Republic of Germany's Distinguished Service Cross and the Vietnamese Cross of Gallantry (with Silver Star). For two tours of duty, he served in Vietnam as a helicopter pilot.

A graduate of Tuskegee Institute, Alabama in 1960 with a Bachelor of Science degree in mathematics and biology, he earned his Master's of Business Administration degree from Atlanta University in 1971, graduating first in his class, and was also graduated from the Senior Managers in Government Program at the Kennedy School of Government at Harvard University. He is also a graduate of the U.S. Army's basic and advanced engineering programs, the command and General Staff College, and the prestigious Army War College.

A native of Wedgeworth, Alabama, Williams, 51, is married to Marjorie Seymore, a former school teacher. They are the parents of two sons and one daughter.

Maj. Gen. CHARLES E. WILLIAMS

Eight

Helping the Children

A daunting task by any measure! I was interviewed by many officials including the Mayor Koch and was determined to be the choice to become the first President/CEO. In this capacity, I had the big job of setting up the organization that quickly grew to over 600 personnel. My reporting chain of command was to a three member trustee board. One trustee was appointed by the Governor, one by the Mayor and the school Superintendent also served as a Trustee. It was a very unusual arrangement as this authority was replacing a long standing government staff and obviously this new authority was not well received. The trustees played a very heavy hand into the operations of the authority (particular the Governor's appointee). This arrangement was simply a no win situation for a newly hired President and CEO from the outside. So, yes we had our share of turf issues over staff appointments, who were really in charge and etc.

In spite of all of this organizational interference, we were able to hire some decent staff very quickly and got the organization off the ground in record time. It not only got off the ground but we were able to meet our goal for production/execution for the first two years. Our budget for the first five years was over $4 billion, and almost every school had to be replaced or undergo major renovations.

The major challenge was not working in New York City or finding quality consultants and contractors but wrestling with the Trustees on personnel selections, contractors and consultant's selection and more. It was a very difficult situation for almost three years but through it all we did good work for the children and they were so thankful for the effort.

I will attempt in the next few pages to take you on a tour of what we were able to do and the challenges encountered. To begin, most all of my Vice Presidents were selected by the trustees prior to my arrival and one of the Vice Presidents had worked as a deputy for one of the trustees on a previous job. The trustees had other mid-level staff that they asked me to hire as well. I was able to attract a few good people to help me but they were not in the senior most positions. The location of our temporary and permanent offices was selected by the trustees as well. The long-standing Wick's Law that required multi-prime contractors on construction projects was lifted for the project and that was major step in the right direction. There was much discussion over which consultant to hire and for what throughout my tenure. In a nutshell, it was a very difficult arrangement for me but in spite of all of this, we were able to launch the programs and exceed our performance target for the first and second years. The principals, teachers and students were extremely proud and many of them were vocal about the help that we were bringing to the facilities side.

The New York Times
Metropolitan News

NEW YORK, NEW JERSEY, CONNECTICUT/MONDAY, MAY 21, 1990

Ex-General's Spit-and-Polish Way to Build New Schools

By JOSEPH BERGER

Almost a year ago, Charles E. Williams traded a two-star Army general's hat for a gray hard hat, and now he spends much of his days at school construction sites, surrounded not only by dust and rubble but also by an air of hope.

The general, as his associates call him, has been assigned the imposing job of building 50 new schools and 30 annexes and remodeling 70 other schools for a New York City system that is badly overcrowded and decaying. He has been given $4.3 billion, but only five years to do this.

School construction has historically suffered huge delays and cost overruns, and the workmanship has generally been shoddy. But the general has quickly established a reputation for a kind of spit-and-polish discipline and for wresting command of construction from the bureaucrats and private contractors. Not a single job is behind schedule, he says, and several are ahead of schedule.

'How to Work, How Fast'

"We just don't have behind schedule in our vocabulary," the Alabama-born Mr. Williams said, with characteristic self-confidence. "I'm going to tell you when to work, how to work, how fast to go. If you want my contract, this is the way you have to go."

Officials at the Board of Education, from Joseph A. Fernandez, the chancellor, to Robert F. Wagner Jr., the president, said they have been impressed. In his nine months as head of the New York City School Construction Authority, Mr. Williams has started construction or renovation of more than 20 schools. In the last decade, the Board of Education, striving to recover from the city's fiscal crisis, opened only 14 new schools and 15 "mini-schools" or annexes.

Mr. Williams's crisp approach was evident on a recent tour of three sites in Manhattan and the Bronx. At each, he cajoled or

Continued on Page B7

Charles E. Williams, left, a former Army general who has been assigned the job of building 50 new schools and 30 annexes and remodeling 70 others in New York City, at a construction site in the Bronx with Shelly Silifstein, the project manager.

A Spit-and-Polish Approach Builds New Schools

Continued From Page B1

charmed his project managers, pushing them to shave weeks off the deadline.

"I want the pupils to have the school as a Christmas present," he told Al Sergany, who was supervising an addition to Public School 152 at 93 Nagle Avenue in Washington Heights. The annex, which will allow the overcrowded school to take 300 extra students, is scheduled to open in January.

Felicita Villodas, the principal of P.S. 152, thanked Mr. Williams for canceling work on a day students needed quiet to take their citywide reading tests. Later, at a renovation at DeWitt Clinton High School, William Dougherty, the assistant principal, complimented Mr. Williams's managers for consistently giving the school enough notice to juggle classroom schedules.

'Complete Turnaround'

"I have been through a modernization before and all the horror stories you've heard about are true," Mr. Dougherty told Mr. Williams, referring to Clinton's renovation 22 years ago. "So I appreciate the complete turnaround that has taken place."

If the general has been criticized, it was for the salaries he has been paying. The general is paid $145,000 and three vice presidents are paid $110,000. But Mr. Williams said he must pay salaries comparable to private industry to get people "who understand design, construction, who are credible."

"If I want a Chevrolet, I'm going to get it," he said in a recent interview. "If I want a Cadillac, I've got to pay the price. And I feel the kids in this town deserve the best. I'm determined to have people on board as talented as those who work for Trump or Tishman or any of the other long-ball hitters in town."

The authority was created by the State Legislature in December 1988 as an independent agency that would take over from the Board of Education the job of designing and building public schools. Its financing was patched together through New York City general obligation bonds and from Municipal Assistance Corporation funds.

It typically takes 8 to 10 years to select and to obtain approval for a site and, then, to design and to build a school. To cut that time in half, the Legislature permitted the authority to forgo land-use reviews and a host of other preconstruction steps, and it let the authority eliminate undesirable contractors from the bidding pool.

Most significantly, it exempted the authority for five years from the Wicks Law, which requires municipal agencies to hire separate contractors for plumbing, electricity and heating instead of having a general contractor in charge of the work. The Wicks Law has been criticized for crippling construction by failing to place anyone in charge. There are stories of painters and plasterers completing their work, and electricians then coming in to make holes for the wiring.

In a report last month, the City Bar Association in New York suggested that the Legislature did not go far enough, and that loopholes still limited

> 'We just don't have behind schedule in our vocabulary.'

the authority of the prime contractor.

Nevertheless, Mr. Williams believes he has been given enough power to do the job on time. He feels he will be able to get around cumbersome union work rules. "You have to demand performance," he said. He has been firm with contractors, who he says, have occasionally tested his "spine."

He will not tolerate too many change orders — authorized changes, for renegotiated amounts, to the original job specifications — that can allow low-bidding contractors to reap windfalls. And he will not let work get bogged down in disputes over change orders.

He will, he says, pay his contractors on time, instead of following what he suggests has been the board's laggard record. And he will not, he says, be drawn into the corruption that has marred the industry.

"I don't accept the old myth that you have to accept a little dirt," he said. "I'm a steward of the public dollars and I will not accept any gouge on those dollars. Once you accept it, you're hooked."

His secret, he says repeatedly, is to have his lieutenants stay on top of each job and not relinquish authority to the contractors. Designating one manager for each site, he said, allows him to lay the blame correctly when things go wrong.

"I'm not sure there was enough vigilance," he said of the board's building program. "Industry does not control the job, we do."

The 51-year-old Mr. Williams, born in the rural town of Wedgeworth, Ala., learned construction from his father, a subcontractor whose assignment it was to clear the timber and earth before the excavators came. At age 10, Mr. Williams started working for his father, but he went on to graduate from Tuskegee Institute, and in the middle of his military career, he earned a master's in business administration from Atlanta University.

A Pilot in Vietnam

He spent 29 years in the Army Corps of Engineers, at first as a helicopter pilot in Vietnam ferrying engineers under enemy fire to repair roads or install wells. Later he directed huge projects in Europe and the United States, including the construction in the mid-1980's of a $1.3 billion, 3,000-acre addition to Fort Drum in New Watertown, N.Y.

None of his current projects, taken alone, are that big, but many are as complicated. Clinton, in the north Bronx, is undergoing a $30 million modernization that requires the building of 17 temporary classrooms to accommodate students shifted out of sections being revamped.

"The construction authority seems to be in tune with the way private construction works," said Michael Manniello, the supervisor for HRH Construction, Clinton's prime contractor. With other municipal agencies, he said, "you send a letter and it sits on 14 desks and no one makes a decision."

In an industry that has been short on black, Hispanic, and Asian workers, Mr. Williams, who is black, has his own way of bolstering the number of minority contractors and employees.

"Percentages, goals and targets are a phony," he said. Instead, he believes in personally talking to contractors and letting them know how important he sees the employment of minority builders for a largely minority school system. He also gives them a list of minority contractors with proven records.

"When you flash a quota at me, you're not forcing me to change my behavior," he said. "I want you to go inside yourself and fix the problem."

Of the $200 million in contracts awarded to date, 18 percent have gone to minority contractors. At most sites, his office said, more than 30 percent of the work force is made up of minority workers.

Mr. Williams has taken a strong stand in negotiations over the 150 designers, engineers and other employees who the authority will be absorbing from the Board of Education. Mr. Williams is demanding a thirty-seven-and-a-half hour workweek from any transferred employees, rather than the 35 hours to which their union contract now binds them.

"The people must understand they will play by my rules," he said. And then conscious of the firmness of his tone, he said, "This is a tough town and, I can tell you, a wimp won't make it."

It was very encouraging to visit schools and the communities and hear the comments and supportive words in speeches and to me personally. This kept me going in as much as all this effort was to make it better for the children and the communities. I knew from military experience that the quality of the facilities made a big difference in how a young soldier reacted to his/her job and most of all the positive impression it had on the young families. Our method of management was to put in place on site at the school a talented manager to run the job. The first school to be modernized was PS 279 in the Bronx. The entire school interior was gutted and given a completely new inside. I recall this first effort cost around $26 million.

The NYC School Construction Authority broke ground last Wednesday on a $5.7 million one-story mini-school at PS 55 in Richmond Hill. While the new structure is under construction, the SCA will modernize the existing building. From left: (background) City Councilmembers Karen Koslowitz and Morton Povman; School District 28 community superintendent C. Raseh Nagi; school principal Norman Weisman; (foreground) Deputy Borough President Peter Magnani; Richmond Hill resident Kristine Velazquez, who will attend the first class of the new mini-school; and General Charles Williams, president and CEO of the SCA.

Since this was a new authority that was replacing a long standing Government organization, it was not an easy "change management" effort. We were careful to do each job the best we could under the existing conditions as this change took hold. The location of suitable sites to build new schools was a big task and there were very few that did not need some type of environmental restoration and extensive site work. Our design and the requirements for the academic work were at the top end and this lead to production of a good state-of-the-art facility. My schedule during the first year was almost unbearable with appearances, speeches, etc. This type of schedule was necessary to get to know the key players and to be seen in the community. I tried hard to put in place a good team that could do the job and create an environment for the consultants and contractors that was friendly and professional. The media was all over our work and I rated it fair in most of its presentation.

My wife and I did find time to locate and attend a wonderful church in Brooklyn, Concord Baptist Church, and the theater to take in some of the quiet social activities in New York City. I gave speeches to countless industry groups and was selected as the sub-contractors' public official of the year, was the Whitney Young Community Service Award recipient and one the Engineering News Record's "Markman" Award in 1991. I tried to stay connected to my many friends in the Army Corps of Engineer by attending some of their events as well. My Public Affairs Officer, Pam Snook, was always on top of her game and did a superb job in assisting me in this area. She was well versed in the New York setting and very keen on her way around the city.

I recall that the high schools had a requirement for Astro Turf Football fields, very wide hallways and state of the art classrooms each being computer ready. We did tackle some of the system's most historical and delicate facilities (i.e. Dewitt Clinton, Morris, and Taft in the Bronx; Sarah Hale and Ft. Hamilton in Brooklyn; Midwood in Queens and the music school on 42nd street where the musical "Fame" got it traction in Manhattan. It was without question a very delicate building and rebuilding process. There were many issues in some of the big modernizations like Waldleigh High School in Harlem. Our team came together very quickly and we began to work on a "fast track" schedule to tackle this $28 million renovation. We were able to find enough good contractors and designers to support our big program in the early phases. I was recognized by the children and the teachers at a special ceremony in 1991. This was a very difficult management environment and the program was large and very demanding on a new organization.

There were big challenges in setting up and the keeping school construction authority focus. Since this first of its kind with a $4.3 billion budget that had essentially replaced the traditional governmental staff was not favored by all. I mentioned earlier in this chapter of the players and the politics. There were much of both at play in the beginning to tackle the core issue of transformation or "change." My honeymoon of about 120 days initiatives soon ended and at the end of my first year, there were some budget reduction in the state and city. While I had been assured that our construction and renovation budget for this critical effort would not be cut, there were suggestions of some reductions. The one budget reduction that the Trustees offered up was salary reductions of the senior staff at the School Construction Authority (SCA). This was very unsettling for me and I expressed my opposition and concern for this action because it was one of my pivotal questions, I had prior to accepting the job. This obviously did not hold well with the Trustees and as a result our relationship began to erode. I worked hard to minimize this issue and keep the ball rolling but as would be expected, it did not go away very easily.

n. Charles Williams visits one of SCA's 500 projects.

News conference following a site visit to NYC School Project.

We continued to work hard and received much praise from the students, teachers and principals. One principal stated in tears at a completion ceremony that I had done what we said we would do and it was going to make a difference in the students' ability to learn. We were encouraged by the number of contractors who were participating and winning the contracts. Our minority and disadvantaged participation was also very well represented in all of our work, and this was known throughout the community. We had a good staff and they were fair and in my view got the job done in a very professional manner. The city officials in each Borough were very kind toward me and understood the transformation process we were bringing. The city council presented me with a proclamation for my service as I was nearing the end of my tenure as President and Chief Executive Officer and this meant so much to me.

I made it a specific point to deal with all our contractors and consultants very professionally and I believe they respected me and the positions I took around all issues. Over the course of my tenure as President and CEO, I had received several offers for other job opportunities. I had not even considered any until the opportunity to manage the building of the first private toll road in Virginia in 150 years came along. I had always enjoyed challenging assignments and responsibilities and this opportunity presented that level of interest. After I agreed to accept the new responsibility and to return to Virginia to serve as the Chief Operating Officer for the private toll road organization (TRIP II).

The New York Times
Metropolitan News

NEW YORK, NEW JERSEY, CONNECTICUT / TUESDAY, SEPTEMBER 26, 1989

Ground Broken for First School Planned by New Authority

Local officials broke ground near overcrowded Public School 79 in the Bronx for the first school, P.S. 279, to be built by the New York City School Construction Authority, which was created to speed school construction. Evelyn Rodriguez, 10 years old, who told the group how she had been consulted on the school's design, was helped as she spoke at the ceremony by Charles E. Williams, president of the authority, and Dr. Fred Goldberg, left, superintendent of School District 10. The State Legislature created the authority last December and gave it powers to cut through red tape.

Paradigm Shift – How We Did It

Since there had been so many negative reports on how the school facilities were managed through the years, and a lot of expectations for the newly created school construction authority, it was only natural that the residents and students, administrators, and contractors would be providing feedback and making evaluation. So, during the beginning of the second year such evaluation or score card was provided and presented. It pointed out that the people were seeing the difference in how the school construction was being planned and managed. I observed that the worried principals began to contact me and other elements in authority about their new buildings. Politicians met me over breakfast. Workers introduced themselves at job sites. Scores of contractors that had stayed away from city work were coming back to the authority to bid on its project.

The authority's orders were to rebuild much of the city's deteriorated system of school buildings by spending $4.3 billion over five years. Fair play and a level playing field have always been part of my management style, so during the first 6 months of my tenure as President/CEO, I worked tirelessly to ensure that if nothing else was recorded about my stewardship it would be clear to all that I was able to create fair working and business environment. I knew we couldn't make this big job go without total support of industry, so I said, "I'm going to be fair with you, and you be fair with me." Fairness went far in New York City, where contractors were accustomed to butting heads with unresponsive or hostile bureaucrats at city agencies. That had been the case with the Board of Education in previous years. The old system appeared to have little regarded whatsoever for the cost of construction, even when it took an inordinate amount of time to complete through no fault of the contractor.

Our management focus was to take the opposite approach. Potential bidders were subjected to a rigorous pre-qualification procedure. Lopsided terms were left out of contracts. Bills were paid promptly, and inquires from contractors with problems were answered swiftly. If things came to an impasse, disputes were arbitrated before a resolution board whose composition was considered a model of fairness. At that time, we had contracts worth $900 million and had assumed control of work in progress worth another $400 million. We were on budget and on or ahead of schedule on every job and there were many of them. We had started 45 projects since getting to work in July 1989, including 13 new schools, 19 renovations, four additions and nine athletic fields. There was much more work to be done and I wanted to see more reputable companies chasing after it. We estimated that there were more than 100 firms bidding on our jobs, many had never before performed school work for the city of New York. Of those, over 80 were either serving as construction managers or contractors.

We modeled our management preamble around the best practices in private-sector construction. For an example, almost every project had a full-time staff project manager and some had outside construction managers. We paid our staff slightly more than typical government construction salaries. In addition, we instilled an esprit de corps utterly lacking in other city construction bureaucracies. I suggested that our success may win the right to continue after the initial five-year budget expired and that its methods may be applied to other public agencies in New York and elsewhere. I had a sense that we had made believers out of a lot of people and as much as the *Engineering News Record* "ENR" had produced an article "New York City School Construction Authority (SCA) earns high grades" about that same time. Recognition of this new paradigm shift in dealing with industry, I was selected as public official of the year by the subcontractor's association a few months prior. This was obviously in honor and one of the few awards along "My Road" that I sincerely cherish.

The sadness of leaving was never shown to the public (only to my close family) but I can say today that I had mixed feelings about my decision. The one big reason I had some mixed emotions was the fact this was a first of its kind organization and I was the first leader of a new organization that was established by State Legislature in December 1988 to meet an urgent need to build and rebuild schools in New York City. This needed an independent organization capable of speeding-up and improving the process of designing, building and rebuilding the public schools. Our objective was to carry out the mission by following a careful crafted five year capital plan that was prepared and approved by the New York City Board of Education for Fiscal years 1990-1994. The results were carefully recorded in an annual report that was made public. It showed in late 1991, a few months prior to my departure the following facts:

- The Trustees reported that the New Cty School Construction Authority's second fiscal year had been extremely successful.
- The Trustees also quickly pointed out that Fiscal 1991 had been an extremely difficult year for all level of government. The city and state had struggled through several fiscal crisis and the

entire country was in a recession.

- I pointed out in the same report that as the authority begins its third year it was directing a program of more than $1.9 billion and doing its job in a cost effective manner, on schedule and with a superlative safety record.

- The facts were:
    - ✓ Pre-qualified 1,663 firms to do work for SCA
    - ✓ Registered $1.3 billion in new construction related contracts
    - ✓ Completed three new mini schools
    - ✓ Completed one addition
    - ✓ Completed one modernization
    - ✓ Completed three additions/modernizations
    - ✓ Completed 841 capital improvements
    - ✓ Completed five athletic fields
    - ✓ Introduced the implemented standards construction specifications
    - ✓ Managed more than 1,000 construction/consultants contracts
    - ✓ Introduced a computer-aided drafting and design system
    - ✓ Introduced a computerized management information system
    - ✓ Managed a program exceeding $1.9 billion.

Ground-breaking for P.S. 279.

rops Fallin' on Our Heads!

Let the school year begin -- P.S. 398 Principal Debra Braithwaite, assistant principal Debra Braithwaite, assistant principal Rose Marsalez, City Council President Andrew Stein, Mayor David Dinkins, Gen. Charles Williams, assistent to Borough President Howard Golden Gail Hammerman, and assistent to Councilman Enoch Williams Keith Cormier grin as they cut a ribbon marshalling repairs completed at P.S. 398.

Law, which requires government agencies to hire separate contractors for plumbing, electricity and heating, the SCA was able to hire one general contractor, the New York Roofing Company, to repair P.S. 398.

Ribbon Cutting Ceremony

The New York City School Construction Authority held ribbon-cutting ceremony for the first school completion in Manhattan : a $3.3 million mini school designed to accommodate 168 kindergarten students in the borough's Washington Heights/Inwood section. From left: NYS Assemblyman Herman D. Farrell, Jr.; Guillermo Linares, President of School Board 6; NYS State Senator Franz S. Leichter; NYC Councilman Stanley Michels; General Charles E. Williams, President and Chief Executive Officer of the SCA; Principal Blanca Battino; Marvin Higgins, Chairman of Community Board 12; Anthony Amato, Superintendent Community School District 6; Doris Gonzalez-Light, Chancellor's Representative and Luis Reyes, Manhattan Member of the Board of Education. In front of them are Indhira Polanco and Wilpani Oleio, future students of the mini school.

School Construction Authority Completes $3.3 Million Mini School

Retired General Charles E. Williams, President and Chief Executive Officer of the New York City School Construction Authority (SCA), announced this week that the Authority has completed its first school: a $3.3 million mini school designed to ease severe overcrowding in Manhattan's Community School District 6, the borough's most overcrowded school district.

It is also significant to state clearly that our independent accountant (Price WaterHouse) concluded its work in 1991 and stated that the organization was in conformity with generally accepted accounting principles. This first job following my retirement from the U.S. Army was registered as a major sign post on "My Road."

My resignation from the school construction was not a complete surprise as my working relationships with the existing Trustees were not the best for me. The resignation was viewed by me as a win-win for both sides. I made my rounds to offer my thanks and good bye to all the wonderful people who had done so much to help me start up this new organization. This was the toughest task for me since we were doing so well, the new 600 person staff was working as a team and the customers were generally happy. I felt much pain because this organization was the house that "Chuck" built. The first 120 days were very tough as I had to put the organization together and got it going for operation in the shortest time ever. We worked night and day and made it, and the team bonded. On the eve of my departure from the school construction authority, I will admit now that it was a tough decision. I had left the Army when I was doing very well to go to New York City to help the children. This was truly my motivation to leave the Army early and I was glad "My Road" took me in a direction where I could help the children.

For the new job in Virginia, I was interviewed by the majority owner, Magalen O. Bryant, a very smart and intense lady. She started the interview by saying that she knew all about me and that she was here to make me an offer to join her in building the first Private Toll Road in Virginia in 150 years. My wife was not exactly thrilled to leave Virginia to come to New York in the first place, so this was welcome news to her. We discussed it and made the decision to take the job and return to Virginia. Since we were in a government house prior to departing and our house was rented, we had to find a rental and begin the process of building a new home in Loudoun County near the job. The chores associated with finding and working the issues associated with a new home being built consume much of my wife's time during the early months of our return to Virginia. After we settled down into the rental in Loudoun County, I reported for duty in my new job. This event represented a big climb for "My Road" toward the top. It was innovative and laced with much lash-up work with the state of Virginia and the local management effort authorities in Loudoun County.

It did not take long for the local business and public officials to learn that the manager for the building of the Toll Road was in town. I was seeking so much help and assistance quickly. The majority owner of the private firm, Mrs. Bryant ensured that I was introduced around to all the key people in Loudoun County. Our offices were in Leesburg, VA, very near the historical court house. It was a nice place to work in an old town that had been touched with modern growth facilities. The project was stalled and there was not much progress when I assume responsibility as Chief Operating Officer.

In addition to this new and large responsibility, I was approached by the President of Shenandoah University, Jim Davis, about the notion of serving as an adjunct professor of Business (but on the Leesburg, Virginia campus). I was always thinking how I could really use the academic side of my MBA degree and the two years that I taught during the evenings was a great experience. I was later offered an opportunity to serve on the Board of Trustees of Shenandoah University…a great experience and another big sign post on *My Road*.

Nine

First Private Toll Road in Virginia in 150 years

I felt very fortunate to have been selected to manage this history-making project, not only for those who sponsored the Dulles Greenway, but also for our nation and the state of Virginia because the Dulles Greenway was the first of its kind in more than 100 years. I do not know how history will treat this type of project, but it had been a long time since anyone had a complete delivery of a privately owned toll road in the state of Virginia.

The story of the Dulles Greenway is a very long one. September 29, 1993, was the day we broke ground. The Dulles Toll Road runs about 14.1 miles westward from the Dulles Airport to the town of Leesburg, Virginia. In September 1995, just 24 months later, we cut the ribbon—celebrating the opening of the Dulles Greenway Toll Road.

The Dulles Greenway Toll Road.

Why the Fast Track

One of the major concerns of government then was the inability of the public sector to deliver infrastructure improvements due to a lack of available funding from taxing and bonding sources. The infrastructure needs of the Nation required bold new creative thinking to break the paradigms of the past. While the Dulles Greenway was specifically an example of public-private cooperation in the development of new infrastructure (with environmental commitment extending throughout construction and the life of the project) such a cooperative approach was increasingly being advocated by leading-edge, progressive thinkers on many fronts, including education, the environment, and health care.

The development of the Dulles Greenway, a 14.1 miles extension of the existing State owned Dulles Toll Road which would connect Dulles International Airport to Leesburg, Virginia had many obstacles and hurdles to overcome. It takes time for the seed of any new innovative idea to grow and the Dulles Greenway was no exception. Magalen Bryant, the visionary for this road never gave up during the seven long years of struggle. Mrs. Bryant led the charge and always said, "when you hit a barrier, go over, under or through, never stop" and she would not let any of the team even slow down. Her faith in the concept of public-private partnerships and this project pushed all the parties involved, government, financial institutions, investors and local citizens towards the goal of ground-breaking of this monumental transportation project. Virginia's Lieutenant Governor Don Beyer told the audience in attendance at the ground-breaking that, "This project has been pronounced dead more often than Elvis has been seen alive."

Ground-breaking ceremony.

At the ground-breaking on September 29, 1993, over 950 of the business, civic, political leaders and general public met to begin the great journey of building the first private toll road in Virginia since 1816. "A major step has been taken towards the completion of the Dulles Greenway with the commitment of financing for the project. The private financing and construction of this road represented a new paradigm for cooperation between the public and private sectors in addressing our public funding for needed transportation projects. This commission recommended and the General Assembly passed the Virginia Highway Incorporation Act of 1988, which removed the state prohibition on private toll roads and set public policy to encourage construction of safe, economically viable highways by private parties. After this legislation was in place, we had to receive approvals from the Virginia Department of Transportation (VDOT) on roadway alignment and construction plans as the road had to be constructed to VDOT standards. The State Corporation Commission had to review all financial documents and approve the toll rates and grant the 42.5 year franchise to operate the road. Locally, TRIP II had to amend the Loudoun County Master Plan and obtain a Special Exception from the County to allow for construction.

Ground-breaking Ceremony - Dulles Greenway Toll Road.

The Dulles Greenway project was planned in a manner sensitive to the environment and other community considerations. During the planning process, we worked very closely with environmental experts to establish a strategy that would minimize disruption to the local environment. Our commitment extended throughout the construction and will continue through the life of the project. This commitment to environmental stewardship in designing and building the new highway represents a dramatic departure from traditional road building. A specialist in urban and environmental planning was hired at the onset to ensure the construction project met or exceeded all local, state and federal requirements ranging from wetlands protection to erosion and sedimentation control.

The U.S. Army Corps of Engineers used the Greenway's wetlands mitigation project, the largest in Virginia, as a national model. While the construction of the Greenway would result in the loss of about 64 acres of federally-protected wetlands, the Building Green program of TRIP II provides for replacement of 149.65 acres in a single, viable site. More than 23,000 native hardwoods, shrubs and grasses were individually planted in April 1994. The site was monitored for five years.

The road design and construction was also protective of Goose Creek, a state scenic river. Engineers designed a more expensive clear span bridge to place piers on shore, avoid the turbidity problems associated with in-water piers and keep work crews out of the creek bed. The Goose Creek Scenic Advisory Committee provided invaluable assistance in river protection efforts. This group was one of the many environmental and civic groups who were consulted by TRIP II so that the community was a part of the process.

The Dulles Greenway captured the state-of-art for smart highways in the United States. It included an Automatic Vehicle Identification (AVI) system coupled with other high tech innovations that was designed to ensure that the road was a pioneer and leader for the century ahead.

One of the things we learned early on about a successful toll road was that the road has to leave one rather significant point and connect to another one. In our case, it starts at Dulles Airport, which was the airport at that time with the greatest capacity to expand on the East Coast and had a $2 billion capital program planned. So it made good strategic sense to connect a road to that significant facility. Beyond that, the Dulles area was a dynamic growth area for a lot of reasons that made this area the ideal location. The Air and Space Museum was moving to that vicinity, so this also factored into some of the corporate thinking. We connect the road to Leesburg, a town which has historical significance and it was also growing. That was, overall, the fundamental strategy that went into the corporate planning on selecting the location for the road.

There was already a pressing public need for an infrastructure facility of this type. Let us look at a couple of reasons. Number one, the state needed to unload traffic off the lateral north roadway, which was Route 7, and the southern lateral of Route 50 and Interstate 66. At the same time, that particular portion of the county offered the best opportunity for growth because in and around the Washington area the other corridors are approaching maximum development. Therefore, the Dulles corridor seemed to offer the best opportunity as economists were telling us at the time. The strategy for locating the road on this footprint was two-pronged. One, it made good strategic sense from the standpoint of planning a transportation corridor. The second critical point was that you do not locate a toll road, or any other transportation facility to which you expect to have user fees attached, just any place. You must really think it through, not only in order to make good transportation and public sense, but also to match the economics.

There were two questions that we thought were very important, one for the public side and one for the private. We had to really think about where we are going to be in the year 2020. We had to think about the whole infrastructure question as it related to transportation in the year 2020, because we simply could not put facilities in place overnight. Delivery of private facilities was very difficult because they were linked to private financing. However, whether the financing comes from the public or private sector, it was still a very difficult business.

Virginia was very fortunate because a lot of money flowed into its transportation coffers. The problem was that some of the $2 billion, in my opinion, was going into the wrong pots. For example, 45 percent of the transportation dollars was going toward new construction at that time and the amount; should have been around 75 percent in my way of thinking. Therefore, the 40 percent required for maintenance, which drains the new dollars, quite frankly was too high. On the other hand, Virginia had a lot of transportation network that was obsolete and needed a tremendous amount of maintenance.

The avenue for the private sector to become a partner was to carve into the maintenance area with new construction and help reduce it to 20 percent. Then the private sector could take a whack at the inefficiencies in the 15 percent in operations by putting in smart highway operating techniques and reduce that to about 5 percent. In my view, the transportation dollar should have been broken out as 5 percent operations, 20 percent maintenance, and 75 percent new construction.

Virginia has many highways and as a result a big maintenance problem. The state estimated it would be spending $40 billion over the next 20 years. Virginia would still be unable to fulfill its total maintenance requirements. This was what drove the whole notion of enticing the private sector to come in and help with the problem because, regardless of which side of the aisle may be driving the political process, you cannot handle this $40 billion problem in the next 20 years without help. This was also why there were very good opportunities in the state of Virginia for private sector infrastructure projects.

These were some of the high hurdles that we had to get over. Securing equity sponsors was a big issue because, obviously, that would be the first dollar spent on this project, and it was the high risk dollar. Equity sponsors were not easy to find because we were talking about soliciting an individual, a pension fund, a bank, or some financial institution to put money at risk and receive a no-book earning for quite some time. So, quite frankly, the sponsors were very selective. There were some out there, but we have to be very mindful that they were not easy to capture.

Local and state agreements were also very important. Environmental work, in my estimation, was at the top of the list of hurdles. You simply cannot finesse the environmental process in a project of this scope. You operate with a deregulated mentality, but at the same time there are certain compliances that you must do because the whole concept of privatization was that you are borrowing a project from the public portfolio and moving it over into the private world for a period of time. We were going to privatize it, operate it like a private entity for a certain concession period, and then it goes back to the public. The responsible public entity, be it a state or a city or whatever, was the ultimate owner of that facility, so we could not ever step completely away from the public arena.

Securing permits and engineering issues are self-explanatory, but it was very important to get the right contractor and have that contractor listen to the new drumbeat. Securing the financing was very difficult. Our project costs were about $326 million using three different types of money: a heavy equity slice; some construction-dollar funding, which we call short-term money; and some 30-year money, which obviously was of the long-term lenders who could stay the course for 30 years.

The end game was simple. No one wanted traffic tie ups, and no one wanted more taxes. The only other option was tolls. The ownership did not make any excuse for the toll rate because we did create an option for the traveling public, not a demand. We had given people an alternative that was a "quality of life" enhancement. If time was important to the motorist, then that must be factored into the decision to pay the toll.

In any case, there were parallel arteries running east and west of our roadway that could carry the traveling public from western Virginia and West Virginia into the Washington area, but they have more than 20 traffic lights. The model travel time on either of those arteries was about 1 hour and 15 minutes from Leesburg to Constitution Avenue in downtown D.C., varying about five minutes depending on whether you are coming from north or south. The model time for the Greenway was about 40 minutes to Washington, D.C. The real issue was whether you want to pay to save time or you would like to stay on the other arteries and fight the traffic.

This project, as I mentioned, was the first of its kind. It was fast paced and very expensive because the sponsors probably had a heavier slice of equity than they would like to have seen. Because this was a pioneering effort, there were a lot of skeptics who questioned whether the concept was going to work; therefore, the equity requirements were a little bit higher.

There was a lot of social/economic fallout over this project. We created more than 500 jobs in the region very quickly and quietly. You do not normally think of a privatization effort doing this sort of thing. We were able to attract blue chip lenders, the top of the line in terms of long-term lenders. This obviously made control and management critical. The schedule had to be made, and, of course, the public used this first project as an outdoor theater because it was something that they had not seen for some time.

We had everything that you could possibly have here in the way of challenges. We had to acquire the right of way for 14 miles. We had no condemnation authority per se. Not one acre, not one inch was condemned by the state. We actually purchased outright a third of the road from 47 different landowners, with individual negotiations to get a 250-foot swath across their property. The other third of the property right of way was obtained through a mutual type conveyance arrangement. The landowner was interested in developing a large residential area, making it convenient to have a road and an interchange at that location. In exchange for that, the landowner conveyed a portion of the property.

The eastern portion was on federal property. We could not purchase federal property and we had to work out some other arrangement. The company had a very long leasehold arrangement with the Metropolitan Washington Airport Authority, whereby they leased the 226-acre swath that we touched. In this part of the roadway, we impacted 64 acres of wetlands, so another critical job was to mitigate for the environmental impact of the wetland. In selecting the wetlands site, we had all of the problems of "not in my backyard." The regulatory process required us to do a two-for-one mitigation. We had to put in place about 126 acres with an assortment of plants and trees to satisfy the requirement. The handling of the planting was very delicate. We increased that to 150 acres because, once we started looking at it, there were some enhancements required to make the site a truly class act. So we made it into an environmental show piece. It was being considered for use now by one of the major universities for science work and other conservation training. So these were the by-products.

Everyone who had dealt with construction knew about "retainage." Retainage was normally a portion or percent of the monthly draw that the owner holds for contingencies until the project is done. One of the innovative spins we put on our deal was that we took the retainage up front from the contractor, and we took it from a source that was not cash. We took a letter of credit. So, during the execution we held a letter of credit from our contractor rather than retaining his cash. This was perceived as an incentive for the contractor because, if the contractor intended to do the job right in the first place, and the cash that was expected was not tampered with, this was obviously better for the company as a whole. This also put us in a better posture with the financing institution because we had our retainage up front. So when the project was presented to the financing institutions, we were able to show the letter of credit to answer the question of how to deal with some of the contingencies.

I think it was also important to manage collateral tasks normally facing the highway contractor. The traditional picture a contractor would normally be faced with was – build 14 miles of road, with a number of many bridges, and by the way, would be asked to do all of these other things as well; relocate the utilities, work the insurance out, handle the wetlands, and the regulatory agencies. We had 176 permits associated with this project, which the contractor would have had to deal with. We worked with 17 regulatory bodies of different sorts – federal, state, county, and town – as well as other interested groups. What we did as the owner was to take all of the risk associated with this collateral work and manage those tasks ourselves. As a result, the contractor had a clear shot at the project. He had just the roadway construction to deal with. All of the tasks that would have created problems were pretty much dismissed away from the contractor because the owner took these away.

And then, of course, the last challenge was the organization of the team. Across the board, I might be the only manager who had fully developed a project of this type from inception all the way through delivery. The Dulles Greenway was opened on its 24-month anniversary to the hour. We broke ground September 29, 1993, at 11 a.m., and cut the ribbon September 29, 1995, at 11 a.m. It was finished six months ahead of schedule, and obviously that early completion potential was an incentive for the contractor.

In the operation and maintenance section of the financing plan, we have reserves for overlay pavement. So the money was already in the financials for the first big expenditure. As to whether the private sector will be more efficient at maintaining highways, we were providing data on that in an empirical way. I think even the state of Virginia will say, after a period of time, that the techniques we used to put the facility in place will most likely reduce the maintenance requirements.

Following next are examples of some of the things we did to help with maintenance. As most people who build these facilities know, there was a range of what you can do in compliance with specifications. We operated at the very top end of the specifications. For example, our roadbed required 12 inches of stone before the asphalt. We treated the second 6 inches with cement to make it stronger. We were within specification without cement, but we chose to treat it with cement. We knew this would have a lasting effect and reduce the maintenance.

We had funding in our financial pro forma to overlay the road every seven years. We were hoping to get close to 10 years between re-paving. We had a pavement-monitoring system whereby we would do a lot of diagnostic work. So the state would receive a lot of intelligence about what was happening as we go along. That was how we envisioned maintenance would be reduced over time.

The Greenway had no public money at all. It was not a public/private venture as you know it, where we had a portion of federal money and some matching amount from the state. This was all private money. I would maintain that this was not the ideal way to do it, but we had to proceed with this plan in order to demonstrate to the state that we were a viable partner.

The Intermodal Surface Transportation Efficiency Act (ISTEA) came along about midway through our project. We were not able to utilize it, but we were clearly looking to it in the future. In a model sense, the way it should work would be through the flexibility ISTEA legislation creates for the states. The state of Virginia, hypothetically, would have to petition the federal government to allow certain allocated funding to Virginia to be used for a private venture. That was the way the ISTEA works, as I understand it. ISTEA came with no money. This was a misnomer when it was suggested. When the bill passed, everybody went with their hands out saying, "Where's the money?" There was no new money.

A reasonable question to ask was, when the return of this roadway back to the public, what do you get from the public? The public contribution was to pass legislation to allow the private sector to do this. The Virginia constitution prohibited the state's good faith and credit from being involved in a private arrangement. They entered with us into something called a comprehensive agreement for handling this project. There were no guarantees for anything. But if, for some reason, we would have faltered along the way and could not have completed the roadway, the public would not have been left with a white elephant. The state had the option to come in and take over.

Virginia did not provide any funding, guarantees, or loans. The right model for this I believe would have had the state make a contribution, but we were facing so many hurdles at the time – breaking paradigms in terms of legislation, moving a very sluggish assembly of politicians from a center in which they had operated for years – it was probably, in defense of Virginia, just too much to ask at the time. The state has since followed through with some super legislation and has been superb to work with. Today, Virginia has the one of best enabling legislations for public/private ventures in the country. They can now make guarantee and in-kind type contributions.

Another question for Virginia was how the state ensures that it was not going to take title to a roadway with huge maintenance requirements after our concession period of 40 years? They were protected through this comprehensive agreement. We had to maintain and operate this facility at no less than the state standards. So, at a minimum the owners would be giving the state back what they would have had if they had maintained it themselves. And to make sure that happens; they had inspectors out with us during the construction and also during the operation to make certain the standards are met.

In trying to extend the maintenance period from every 7 to every 11 years, we were not deferring required maintenance. To meet the requirement for a roadway of this nature, built to our design, the state expected an overlay to the pavement every seven years. We provided for that. We had a pavement monitoring system in place during operation to tell us what was going on. We would not overlay unless there was a reason to overlay, so we prepared about the sixth year to petition the state and say, "Based on all of the data we have collected, it does not make sense for us to do this. Don't you agree?"

Round the clock multi-shifts.

Regarding the toll rate, there are two relevant government bodies in the state of Virginia, the State Corporation Commission, which regulates rates, and the Commonwealth Transportation Board, which regulates policy. These commissions are the arms for the governor, and they made decisions on these matters. The Commonwealth Transportation Board decided how the roadway would be managed, designed, and operated, which are policy issues.

Setting toll rate was a joint decision between the private entity, us, and the State Corporation Commission, and it was negotiated. We had a certain project cost. Obviously the investors, the sponsors, needed an acceptable rate of return because of the front-end risk. A combination of this rate of return, servicing the debt, and operating the road was what set the tolls. We did not break out our funding by task. We had short-term money, which we needed to get the road built. That amount of funding was provided mostly by a consortium of banks. They had limits on the number of years they would loan money. The long-term debt financing was done by another group of financial institutions, like insurance companies, pension funds, etc.

The initial dollars came from the sponsors. These were the persons and the entities who own the toll road. The very first dollars committed to the project were the equity dollars, then the bank dollars, and later the long-term lending dollars. There was an agreed upon cap on the rate of return with the state of Virginia. If the cap was ever reached, the surplus would go into a special account, and the owners would then negotiate about how to deal with that surplus.

In summary, all players, lenders, regulators, owners, contractors, and consultants did a fantastic job on this pioneering effort and should be given proper credit. I was very fortunate to have the opportunity to manage the execution of the project. It was hard work and we broke new ground in management of risk and change management in general. I believe there were lessons left for future toll road burden to consider. Mrs. Bryant and I were selected as Co-Citizens of Year in Loudoun County for our work on this first of its kind project.

Mrs. Bryant and me observing the construction.

Mrs. Bryant breaking the first ground for construction.

Pictured with Mrs. Bryant and her son, Michael at the gala celebrating the opening of the toll road.

The Greenway Story

A PROFITABLE PRIVATE VENTURE

One of the great challenges facing Americans today is how to deliver needed infrastructure improvements without creating an undue burden on the taxpaying public.

In the northern Virginia area, we are acutely aware of the need for infrastructure improvements in the form of additional roads to serve a rapidly growing population.

To address these needs, a vital partnership was formed between the Shenandoah Greenway Corporation, the Italian firm Autostrade International S.p.A., and Brown & Root — the Toll Road Investors Partnership II (TRIP II).

In order to build a road from Dulles International Airport to Leesburg, Virginia, many hurdles had to be overcome. There were environmental concerns, county and town master plans to be considered, and an enormous amount of federal, state and local regulations to meet. By consulting with environmental experts, town and county planners, the Commonwealth of Virginia, and the U.S. Army Corps of Engineers, the Dulles Greenway successfully addressed the concerns of all parties who would be affected by a new road in their area.

With the regulatory hurdles well behind them, construction commenced on September 29, 1993 —and has continued at an awe-inspiring pace. Today, the road opens - six months ahead of schedule - and two years to the day after groundbreaking.

— September 29, 1995

The road in place - 1995.

Helping the Children Again

After I completed the big management task associated with the construction of Dulles Greenway, I received a call from a dear friend and mentor LTG (Ret) Becton) who was on the verge of being appointed as the superintendent of the District of Columbia public schools. LTG (Ret) Becton asked me to come and help him out with the major effort of getting the school facilities under contract. I knew that this was big job that had many issues and it would be difficult to get around the politics and get something done. Because General Becton was a friend, I did agree to come and help but indicated that it would only be help to get things pointed in the right direction but not for the long haul.

When I arrived to help, the District of Columbia Public Schools (DCPS) were in court over fire code violations and almost every roof was leaking and most of the boilers did not function properly. There were indication of years of neglect and additionally there was no capital plan in place. I got some staff on board and began to tackle these multiple pronged problems. The court was the most delicate of matters so we began to try to get those issues under control first. It was a few days before I departed when the DCPS finally got out of the courts. We tackled the leaky roofs and worked night and day to repair or replace all properties that were in need. The heating systems (boilers, etc.) were also big issues for us as well. We did what we could to stabilize the situation in a comprehensive program was put in place. I took this impossible task on for two reasons, (1) to help the children of the District of Columbia, (2) to help my friend with that massive responsibility. I knew from the outset that it was an up-hill battle – but I was willing to try.

I did the best that could be done during the time that I was there and believe today that it really helped the children through a very critical situation. This experience was a big sign post on "My Road" and a real lesson to encounter. There are a few times in life when one must take on a task where the odds of success are clearly against you at the beginning, but in order to help just one child, it was worth all of the effort to walk through the storm again. I would do it all over again to try and make conditions better for a child trying to study and develop.

Ten

The Crown Jewel: Returning Back to the Government

"One Mission, One Organization, One Team."

Overseas Buildings Operations (OBO) is the State Department's overseas property manager and is responsible for its entire overseas buildings operation. OBO acquires real estate, disposes of real estate and designs, builds, refurbishes, and maintains them. OBO has more than 16,000 physical structures in 260 countries around the globe, about $12 billion in real estate.

OBO has strategically reinvented itself to become a Results-Based Organization, focused on its ongoing responsibilities as a good steward of the taxpayer dollars during 2001-2007. This operational revolution, in response to the 1998 bombings of the U.S. Embassies in Dar es Salaam and Nairobi, and reinforced by the terrorism of 9/11/2001, generated a need for a fundamentally new OBO structure and philosophy. And as changing world events dictated new diplomatic responses, the condition of our overseas infrastructure could not be ignored. Many of our embassies and consulates need replacement or rehabilitation because they do not meet current safety and security standards, are overcrowded, or are antiquated.

Being sworn in as Director/COO of Overseas Buildings Operations by Secretary of State Colin L. Powell as my wife, Marjorie holds the Bible.

A Great Leader and Friend: Gen. Colin L. Powell – Secretary of State

True courage is to stand against odds, even when we stand alone.

In 2001, I was appointed to the Director/COO of OBO (which was elevated to Bureau status) in the Department of State by Secretary Colin L. Powell. The mission that was given to the organization and the guidance to me was daunting to say the least. The organization was not performing as expected and the management was under attack from the General Accounting Office (GAO), Office of Inspector General (OIG) and others. Secretary Powell was very keen on this soft spot in the Department and was very focus on getting it under control. He requested and I concurred to join and help out on his transition team in December 2000.

My first task was to conduct an independent assessment of the then FBO and provide him with a recommended way forward. I accomplished this task on schedule and made my presentation and as a result, he made the decision to move the function (FBO) out of the Administration Bureau and make it a stand-alone Bureau. The name would also change to Overseas Buildings Operations (OBO) and the leader would be titled Director and Chief Operating Officer and be Assistant Secretary equivalent. He offered me the job with some very basic guidance. "Go ahead, press the envelop and do whatever is needed to fix the capital planning procedures and operations of the organization." It was a compelling mission, but it was very clear that he wanted me to change the way business was being conducted and get the job done. I accepted his offer and the process of bringing me on board commenced. I was pleased with his guidance because he recognized the problem and gave me the freedom to attack the problem in methods and means that I deemed appropriate. He really did not want me to come to him everyday seeking permission to do my job. I appreciated this and today consider this to have been a great demonstration of his leadership style. It gave me the traction I needed to set the azimuth for change. Secretary Powell is a person that I greatly admire, not only for what he has done for our country, but for the fact that he is just good and decent human being – the one person I could not turn down when he called.

I was appointed and sworn in on March 12, 2001 in Secretary Powell's office. My wife, family, and a few special friends were on hand for this important event. In fact, we left home in such a rush without taking our favorite Bible for the ceremony. As we were ready for the swearing in, I begin to sweat a little because I discovered that we had left the Bible at home. Secretary Powell was very cool and calm about this and said, "Oh, Chuck you can use my old Bible that I have carried around with me for years if you desire." It was clear to me and the family that he wanted to get this process over so I could get to work as soon as possible. The swearing in and Secretary Powell's remarks were inspiring and gave me the lift that was needed to dive into what turned out to be the toughest and most visible job in my professional life. This was indeed the sign post on "My Road" that indicated to me that I was really on the super highway with many lanes. These were all fast lanes and everyone on these roads were traveling at maximum speeds. And, failure was not an option.

I waded quickly into the thick of things by starting with an off-site meeting with the senior staff of the organization. It was at this session where I discussed the need for the following:

- A new organizational framework that would provide a short decision chain and a flat structure
- Clearly define management "sand boxes" to facilitate the fixing of accountability
- A Chief of Staff or Integrator who would keep the "sand boxes" connected and integrated
- Begin to use the Principles of Six Sigma to guide the re-organization and operating structure

- Put in place a robust Project Planning and Development sand box to eliminate the dysfunctional Program Management unit
- Initiate a monthly performance review for each program/project in the organization (PPR)
- Put in place an Industry Advisory Panel to keep us keen on Industry Best Practices
- Beef up the Construction Execution Division by adding Commissioning of facilities and better trained project directors
- Make Management Support and Information Management stand-alone and critical functions to keep the organization's engine moving
- Police up all the ragged edges of budget and personnel pieces in each major area and reassigned them to the Resource Management Program Division
- Move to a true Results Based Operation in 120 days and prepare and publish the first Long Range Strategic Building Plan by the end of the year
- Publish an Annual Stewardship Report the first year

I knew this was a big load and was a task to tackle but change was needed and it could only happen through a second curve and just doing it. This change management brought all traditional "push back" but I had to stay the course and drive it in to get the fabric in order to get the organization out of the ditch so that some credibility could begin to grow in the stakeholder views. In December 2001, we were there and were functioning very well. (Not without a few who simply did not want to change).

Eleven

OBO—New Ideas To The Business of Government

This interview provides a clear snapshot of the magnitude of my responsibilities as Director of the Overseas Building Operations. I am grateful to The Business of Government Hour radio program for granting permission to use this interview.

Tuesday, April 6th, 2010 - 10:09
Arlington, Virginia

Mr. Lawrence: Good morning and welcome to *The Business of Government Hour*. I'm Paul Lawrence, partner in charge of the IBM Center for The Business of Government. We created The Center in 1998 to encourage discussion and research into new approaches to improving government effectiveness. You can find out more about The Center by visiting us on the web at www.businessofgovernment.org.

The Business of Government Hour features a conversation about management with a government executive who is changing the way government does business. Our special guest this morning is Major General, retired, Charles Williams, Director of Overseas Building Operations at the U.S. Department of State.

Good morning, General Williams.

Gen. Williams: Good morning, Paul.

Mr. Lawrence: Joining us in our conversation, also from IBM, is Kim Hintzman.

Mr. Lawrence: Well, General Williams, let's start by learning more about the Overseas Building Operations. Could you tell us about the office and when and why it was created?

Gen. Williams: The office was created in order to provide leadership and oversight over the property management in the State Department. The Overseas Building Operation, which has been basically named over the last 3-1/2 years, was put in place in order to provide a sharper focus to the mission and function I just described.

Mr. Lawrence: Can you give us a sense of the approximate value of the owned and leased property under the control of OBO?

General Williams: The portfolio today is about $12 million.

Mr. Lawrence: And the numbers and people who work with you on your team.

General Williams: Well, the number of people that we serve are massive, quite frankly, 40,000 people or so are stationed around the world, 260 separate locations, cities that we serve. We have over 16,000 properties in that whole mass of responsibility.

Mr. Lawrence: And what's the annual operation and management budget to keep these properties?

General Williams: Today, it's slightly under $500 million.

Ms. Hintzman: General Williams, what are your responsibilities and duties as the director of the Overseas Building Operations?

General Williams: That's a good question, because this is a massive responsibility. As I mentioned before, we have 260 locations around the world where we have facilities. My specific responsibility in broad strokes is to manage the property portfolio around buying, selling, leasing, designing, building, and maintaining the facilities that I've just described, and I mentioned that is 16,000.

Ms. Hintzman: So can you describe your organization's relationship with other agencies and organizations?

General Williams: That's a very important point, Kim, and I appreciate the question, because it is often misunderstood that the State Department facility or facilities and the individuals who work in the facilities are not all State Department people. We serve a multitude of agencies. I like to view the facility as a platform; it's a platform from which the U.S. government can project its foreign policy, and that entails the housing of many agencies and activities.

Ms. Hintzman: You've had an honorable career in the Army, and you were retired prior to accepting this position. Can you describe your previous experiences before becoming the director of OBO, and talk about what it was like to go back into the work force?

General Williams: Kim, that's very interesting because I am a recycle, if you will. I kid sometimes with my boss, Secretary Powell, both of us are the same. My previous background, quite frankly, prepared me quite well for this. I was fortunate to have a nice blend of about 30 years in the military, serving in the Army Corps of Engineers, doing exactly what I'm doing now, just a little different spin.

I built a lot of things, managed huge projects. And then, of course, while in the private sector, I was wonderfully blessed to have the opportunity to be chosen to run a very large school program in New York City, a very tough location to do the work; and then, of course, to manage and build the first private toll road in the state of Virginia, the Greenway.

So a combination of these two experiences, and having the opportunity to blend the management concepts of both I think prepared me quite well for this delicate function.

Mr. Lawrence: You went through your background and you talked to us about your different project management experiences. I'm curious how you would compare undertaking large projects in the military and in the private sector.

General Williams: Well, naturally, Paul, they are different, but they are connected in several ways. Project management is project management; you're basically controlling the outcome of a project. The private sector has a sharper closure to its projects because it's more results-based than I would say the time that I served in the military. But having the combination of both and have gone through each one of the experiences, I could see where there's strengths on both sides. The government is very methodical and processed in it. The private sector is more results-based, and of course, durations and time lines are shorter. A combination of all of that makes for a better manager once you have had the experience of going through them.

Mr. Lawrence: How about the decision-making process in both in terms of speed and crispness; how would you compare those?

General Williams: It's interesting, because while in the government, it's process-driven, and the process is a little bit more, I wouldn't say convoluted, but it is crowded. In the private sector, the organization has more of a flat structure, pinpointing responsibility and management sales a little bit easier to connect to the responsible director or leader, and that would be the sharpest contrast. Decision-making in the private sector is quicker, and obviously, the lines are shorter. On the government side, it's a little bit more process-driven and obviously takes a little longer.

Mr. Lawrence: What drew you back to public service?

General Williams: A call from a very dear friend named Colin L. Powell. And if you've not been on the other end of a telephone call when this gentleman calls you, you have no idea what I'm talking about.

Mr. Lawrence: Well, fill us in, what's the line that persuaded you to return?

General Williams: Well, first of all, he is a person that I admire not only as an individual, but as a servant of our country. Paul, he's done an enormous job for our country. I know him; I know his style. It was just a unique situation that he's a few years senior to me in the military, and he had always, for whatever reason, I had always been somewhat associated with things that he either managed or he had been associated with.

When he was Corps commander in Germany, I had the responsibility as a colonel to retrofit all of the new firing ranges in Germany. This was arranged to accommodate our new family of vehicles that was engaged in the Gulf War. So Secretary Powell, then-Lieutenant General Powell, knew of my work at that point. Then, of course, when I was in my division command responsibility, upstate New York, Fort Drum, I had the opportunity to build a complete city. This was a small mini-city, if you will, post, as we call it in the military. The commander who inherited that responsibility was now-Secretary Powell, once again in a position where he could observe exactly what I had done.

And then, of course, when I retired and went back to the private sector, I was in New York City building schools; had a $4 billion budget, lots of schools to rebuild and rehabilitate. One of those schools was in South Bronx, and it was Morris High School. And one of the distinguished graduates of Morris High School was Colin L. Powell.

So I often say this when I'm engaged in discussions like this and interviews or whatever, is that this man probably knows more about what I have done and what I cannot do than anyone. So a long story, to give you sort of an answer as to why he may have called, but I'm proud he did. Mr. Lawrence: Judging from your career, in addition to Secretary Powell, I'm assuming you've been around lots of other really strong leaders, and I'm curious, what makes a leader effective, from your perspective?

General Williams: I think, Paul, this is very good, because I spend a lot of time thinking about leadership, and that's the real foundation I think to making an organization go. An effective leader is a leader that knows how to select people to work with him or her, understand that in order to get the maximum from a subordinate, there has to be mutual trust and respect. In other words, you have to trust a subordinate; you have to cut the subordinate loose and let them run, let them be creative, let them work.

Secretary Powell has a lot of leadership secrets, but one that is very profound, as far as I'm concerned: he gives you a big responsibility, and then he steps back and allows you to do the job. And you do not have to go to him and say, "Boss, can I do this?" He doesn't want you to do that. He wants you to make it happen and then he holds you accountable for the results. That's what makes Colin Powell effective, and that's my construct of an effective leader, and I try to practice that.

Mr. Lawrence: Interesting point, especially about the cutting loose.

The State Department is undertaking a large-scale overseas construction project. What have we learned and why are we doing this? Well, General Williams, the need for substantial investment in secure overseas facilities was tragically demonstrated in August 1998 by terrorist attacks on our embassies in Kenya and Tanzania. How did this experience change the way OBO provides safe and functional facilities for employees and their families abroad?

General Williams: Paul, that is a very interesting question. The horrific incident that occurred that you made reference to woke all of us up to the fact that we had to do things different from the standpoint of standing up our facilities.

We started with hardening the skin, what I call the skin of the building, that is the building structure itself, coupled with providing several layers of perimeter defense arrangements, and this way, this allowed every building that we now are putting in the system to be safer. And I think that made a tremendous difference in the quality of life of our people.

Ms. Hintzman: In the past, U.S. embassies were traditionally focused on consular activities for Americans working and traveling abroad. How has this role changed, and how does this impact the

way that OBO provides services to U.S. employees and their families abroad?

General Williams: Well, I think that, too, Kim, is a very good question, because this allows me the opportunity to explain exactly what we are building. Yes, it is a building, but the building is a diplomatic building which houses many functions, not just a consular operation, but many other functions, like the Department of Agriculture, for an example, that might -- USAID, for an example, who's in a very important role: the CDC, looking at disease and so on. So we have a real collaborative arrangement of concerns and equities now in our building.

Ms. Hintzman: As you mentioned, the embassies are now used as a platform for activities for multiple agencies. I understand that the Capitol Security cost-sharing program is an attempt to pull the resources of agencies to improve the embassy facilities. Can you describe this program, and who's involved in it, and what are the expected outcomes?

General Williams: Good, Kim. I think we have embarked on, with good support from the administration, OMB, and all, on a program that will ultimately get us right in terms of having the resources to correct this major deficiency we have in buildings. By having a cost-sharing arrangement, this allows all of the tenants and partners that I just spoke about that operate and use our platform, for all of us to come together for a short period of time, maybe 10 or 12 years, put our shoulders to the plow, if you will, and provide resources so that we can build quicker.

We have demonstrated I think successfully over the last three years that we have a construct or a management scheme in place now where we can produce facilities quicker and more efficiently. So now is the time for everyone who is involved in this platform that I speak about to come together, and we all push hard. And we can sunset this thing in about 12 years and we'll have the work done.

Mr. Lawrence: Let me take you into some of the decision-making surrounding that. I imagine the CDC, the Department of Agriculture, others, I mean there's probably some sense about, you know, some different opinions about the priorities of the request, the specifications, their security needs; how do you work through that?

General Williams: Well, first of all, we try to do our work up front, the Overseas Building Operation. We came up with standard embassy design templates so that we would take away all of the "we" and the "they" and this type of thing. We made certain that we connected this, going back to my private sector training, to good industry standards. We picked office building standards in the U.S., and so we sized all of our facilities against that standard.

So if you are in CDC or if you are in Agriculture or if you are in the State Department, small issues like room size and conference rooms and this type thing, they're all standard. So by getting everybody on the same page, we then could say that this is not just a State Department building. We have responsibility for running it for the government, but this is our building, and you can see this by looking at things that look alike. So this was the first way of getting everybody on the same page. And from that standpoint, it's working well; this allows us to build the facilities quicker. These standard design products are on the shelf, they are generically designed so that we can pull them off, site adapt them to a particular region around the world, and we cut off months and even years in terms of execution. So we had to demonstrate several things before we could even begin to talk to a tenant about cost-sharing: how quickly can I get it, are you going to be sluggish, will I have the same as you would have? So we eliminated those things up front.

Mr. Lawrence: Let me ask you a question then about the security needs, because I'm imagining some organizations as your tenants would like to have a great deal of interaction with the public, others would prefer none, almost by definition. How do you work through those differences?

General Williams: Well, good question, Paul. I chair a facilities council, and this meets on a periodic basis, where we bring all the tenants in, some 30 or 40 people in a room at one time, and we educate them on the ongoing activities of the program. This is what we're building, this is what's coming next. We give them an opportunity to participate and provide input, ask questions, et cetera.

So this is our way of communicating to those who want information and would like to be involved in the way of input, and offer to those who may not have an interest, so that's our vehicle for that.

Ms. Hintzman: The OBO is embarking on a large-scale overseas construction program; what are the scope and budget for this endeavor; and how does the evolving role of the overseas embassies and the terrorist events impact the execution of these plans?

General Williams: Kim, the program today is robust. 3-1/2 years ago, when Secretary Powell and I came on board, we were looking at sort of a program in the total that produced maybe one embassy new start a year. Over the last 3-1/2 years, with good support from our Congress and OMB, we have now moved that from one to 12 to 15. It's been gigantic progress over the period of time. We are now starting over 10 new embassy compounds per year, and we are cutting ribbons or opening about eight a year.

I think this is sending a very strong signal to those who would want to create problems for us, that we are very serious about taking care of this program. But the most important thing, what it does for our people. I think our people know who serve overseas; they know that we are trying to do our very best to eliminate this problem.

Mr. Lawrence: As you describe the openings and closings, I couldn't help but think that the embassies and the consulates around the world, many must have aged beyond their life expectancy, so I'm curious sort how that came to be just in terms of a management question. And also, are the new buildings being constructed and maintained differently to extend their life spans?

General Williams: Paul, yes, the first question is, we didn't do a good job, and I mean, we, the government, didn't do a good job of watching our portfolio in the past. Our buildings of existing structures are about 40 years old. The useful life of a building almost anyplace is pretty much over at that period of time.

If you compare that to anything else that the U.S. might own overseas, that is about 20 years older than the rest of it, so we have an aging problem, coupled with facilities that did not and do not meet security standards. We are currently expending over -- and plan to spend over a billion dollars a year to build these new facilities and build them quicker and faster.

Mr. Lawrence: You talked earlier about some of the variances or metrics you got from the private sector to sort of influence your thinking. I'm curious in terms of sort of other countries, are they dealing with similar problems with their embassies or are we just very unique?

General Williams: I think we're unique, Paul, from the standpoint of being more vigilant and concerned about this whole matter of secure facilities. We've been hit hard and we know if we do not secure the facilities, what will happen. Our colleagues around the world, and we have good interaction with several of them; they come and visit with us a few times a year, and we do the same. I don't know precisely what they're doing, but we are probably the leader in this secure facilities business at the moment. That's my belief.

Ms. Hintzman: General Williams, upon taking a director position of OBO, you launched a major reorganization; what was your vision of this reorganization?

General Williams: Well, Kim, what we wanted in this new organization was a different focus. We had to build these new facilities very quickly and we had to use a different management technique, and the organizational structure that was in place was not, in my judgment, appropriate for that. Results-based, in broad strokes, means performance and accountability, and having a very flat organization with delineated management cells that would perform certain specific functions; that was the grand scheme of this reorganization.

Ms. Hintzman: So I hear that some of the business drivers are around speed of building and the performance-based, results-based organization; can you describe some of those functions that those cells perform?

General Williams: Yes. For an example, the organization didn't have a robust planning element. Planning is so critical in this business, because we have to plan basically five years ahead, we had to develop and put in place a long-range strategic plan which sort of laid out what we're going to be touching and building over the next five years, and of course, have clearly defined responsibilities for each of the managers.

And we set this up somewhat on a hybrid of what is used in the private sector. My senior managers are managing directors, meaning that each one of the senior persons under me have a management responsibility so that we could capture the accountability and move forward. This is where the combination of my government and private sector experience blended together. I'm using the managing director a la vice president business unit concept from the private sector, and then I'm linking this to a governmental process to build embassies.

Mr. Lawrence: OBO is described as a results-based organization. You've talked to us about the importance of results and accountability. Let's use an example. What does this mean in terms of embassy construction, for example?

General Williams: Paul, what is means is that we are taking a very different approach for building new embassies now. We're not just building an embassy that is a building, we're building compounds, or I like to call them small campuses, because it's built on a 10-acre site; we procure a site that is basically a green site that's not been disturbed or used before; it's not on Main Street, this is a big break from the tradition. This concept will not work downtown; we have to move it out to, in many cases, what is the developing corridor in and around a particular city. We put all of the operating structures that's needed to run an embassy function on this acreage enclosed in a very secure blast-resistant wall, and this is where we end up.

Mr. Lawrence: How are countries reacting to our new approach?

General Williams: Well, they are shocked, obviously, when we start negotiating about property. When we start asking for a minimum of

10 acres, they look very strange because normally, they associate an embassy with one building. But I must admit that we have worked this concept very effectively now for the last three years. We have 27 of these new compounds under construction, soon to have 38, because we have another 11 that we're in the process of putting out as we speak, and this is the new way of doing it.

Using the combination of the standard embassy designs that I described earlier, this is allowing us to basically build one of these campuses in two years versus four and a half years.

Mr. Lawrence: Interesting. Let's go back to the OBO and the results-based organization part of our conversation. What are some of the performance measures you're using to determine if your office is meeting the objectives?

General Williams: Well, one that is used externally is used by the OMB. OMB has a program assessment rating tool called PART. This is where -- it's a very effective tool. It's based, quite frankly, on the results, or said in another way, did you do what you planned to do or what you said you would do? I must say that it is a very tough evaluation arrangement. OBO enjoyed this last rating period on its new facilities, the ones we just finished speaking about, a 97 percent rating. This is one of the highest in the government for performance and effectiveness. And for an organization that was basically in the ditch, if you will, 3-1/2 years ago, we are quite proud of this. And it shows I think once again the importance of the restructuring, the reorganization, and some of the new approaches that we're taking.

Mr. Lawrence: Are there other measures of success besides the PART scores?

General Williams: Well, yes; we have put in place, which I think is, again, the blend of the private sector and the government experience. I have an industry advisory panel. This panel is made up of nine members from industry, very senior members. They meet with me quarterly and my senior staff and they basically advise and sanction any new approach that we're taking.

So once we launch a new program, a new direction, we know that this program will stand the test of industry, such as our standards dealing with the cost-sharing mechanism and this type of thing. So this industry advisory panel, too, has been a winner for best practices, it's been cited by Gallop and others as being one of the most effective advisory apparatuses in the Washington area.

Ms. Hintzman: General Williams, you've talked about a leader holding their people accountable, and we've also been talking a lot about performance measures. In this kind of geographically diverse organization, how do you instill accountability and reward performance?

General Williams: Well, Kim, you hit the nail on the head. You must demand results, but you also -- and this is where the effective leader comes in -- you must reward those who participate. We're big on awards, as we are on results. We take time to set aside twice a year an awards recognition time where we bring all of the persons in who have gone over and above what we expect them, and we make awards.

We tie all of the ratings and the performance evaluations to performance. Our performance measures flow from the managing office down to the division down to the branch, so there's no misunderstanding about what we all mean. For an example, everyone in the organization knows that the time on the clock for delivery of one of the compounds that I've just described is 24 months. We advertise that, we even tell the contractors and all of the private sector partners who work with us. There is no secret, nothing magic about our work. It's all about performing and delivering. So not only does my organization know it, even the private sector partners as well. And that is very effective, and we have a very strong awards program that integrates that.

Ms. Hintzman: It's been very interesting hearing you talk about the new compounds. Now, what are some of the other unique challenges that you face in trying to buy, lease, or build, and maintain U.S. properties in foreign countries?

General Williams: Kim, this is tough work, you know, working in every region in the world. I have personally visited over 100 of these locations myself. It's very difficult, because in many of the countries, the rules for doing business are sometimes not fully developed, so we have to work in that sort of situation. In other countries they are different from what we use here in the United States.

But our people have been exposed and trained in such a way that we now understand how to operate and deal in those particular countries. We still have hard work pushing, zoning, and the acquisition of property and the like through, but we know that it's hard work, so we give ourselves sufficient time and work through it. I can't tell you that it's easy, because it's not. It is very difficult. It compares to nothing that we do here in the United States.

As you know, I managed the construction of the Greenway, and we had 47 land owners, for example, that we had to do real estate business with, very sophisticated Northern Virginia-type land owners, but none of that would even begin to approach the level of complication that we deal with in these foreign countries, because as I said, in many cases, the lines are not clear and the rules are not yet fully vetted.

Well, General Williams, what has OBO done to stand up an interim facility in Iraq since diplomatic relationships have been established there?

General Williams: Well, what we have done, we have put in place several facilities to handle the interim responsibilities. These were stood up very quickly, which allowed our new ambassador and his staff to be ready to take over on the 1st of July of this year.

Mr. Lawrence: How about a permanent facility?

General Williams: A permanent facility is being planned. We are in the process now of looking at properties. It will be a property that will be sufficiently sized to allow us to build a diplomatic community along the same lines that I've described earlier in my interaction here with you. This, we are hopeful, could be launched as early as next year. And once again, we would have a very short duration for completing it.

Ms. Hintzman: General Williams, what other embassies or U.S. facilities in the world are considered to be in high risk areas, and how does the OBO address such security threats?

General Williams: Well, first of all, the identification of what is in a high risk area or what needs to be dealt with from a security point of view is adjudicated by another element in the Department of Diplomatic Security. So we are the doers once the identification of the problem has been cited by diplomatic security.

Ms. Hintzman: And so what is it that you do once they identify those areas where there are high risks?

General Williams: Well, Kim, what we do, first of all, is, our protocol calls for a survey. We survey the particular facility, and as I have mentioned, we have a very standard process in place which allows us to move very quickly to put this particular facility in our strategic plan, and if it's an urgent facility, the plan is flexible enough to move it from the back to the front, et cetera, and then make the presentation through the approval levels, OMB and Congress, and once funding is secured, then we launch the construction.

Ms. Hintzman: We've talked a little bit about the challenges of maintaining buildings around the world; can you tell us a little bit more about some of the benefits and challenges of the Department of State's model of managing its own real estate?

General Williams: Kim, we think we have a very unique method of managing real estate. It's a combination of using the private sector and government; once again blending that experience that I gained by being in both arenas. We have a site search team; it's a global team, international real estate firm, well-heeled in dealing with real estate in these countries. We have a stable of these kind of firms. That's the first part.

The second step would be then to bring in my special real estate team. We have credentialed people on staff, 30 or 40 of them, in real estate, to go in and draw on what the first set of eyes, or the private sector global firm, has found. They isolate around one or two of these, working with the particular embassy post concerns, and come away with a preference of one or number two: bring this back, we make a final decision based on the technical capabilities of the particular site, and then we move to acquire and negotiate the real estate.

We do an appraisal, we do everything that happens here in the United States around price; we negotiate very hard, and end up with, in our opinion, protecting the government quite well.

Ms. Hintzman: We've talked about the industry advisory panel that advises you on a number of different best practices; do you think this is something that you would recommend to other agencies, implementing similar kinds of advisory panels?

General Williams: Kim, I feel so strongly about this particular practice that I would say an organization like the one I'm involved with, I don't believe going forward in the future could survive without this. This has been just a breath of fresh air. These individuals roll up their sleeves; it's pro bono, they are not paid, they are there because they want to be there, they believe in their country, they are happy to support us, they put it all on the line, and quite frankly, help me work through issues. The best way to describe it, it's a big staff meeting. We roll up our sleeves, we brainstorm, and we coalesce around a particular solution, and they go out and support it. I call them my nine ambassadors of the Overseas Building program, because they support it quite well.

Mr. Lawrence: The last couple questions here will draw on your experience. Thinking about your lessons learned in your current role, what advice do you have for other federal leaders who manage large-scale international projects?

General Williams: First of all, the international business is a little tricky, and you have to have an appreciation for the host country's unique rules and the like, and have to find a way to understand that they all will be different. There's some patience we have to be sensitive to, and then, of course, you have to deal in very straightforward business terms to make certain that the end result can be what it should be.

And sort of a summary of all of that is that be very knowledgeable through whatever means and methods you can about the particular region of the country that you're going to attempt to do business. Don't go in cold. Have the right team and the right help, and in many cases, this requires you to draw on well-heeled private sector firms that have been working in the international arena for quite some time to help you work through the maze.

Mr. Lawrence: And while you're giving advice, what advice would you offer to someone just beginning their career in public service?

General Williams: Well, first of all, public service is unique. I frankly think being a person of the background that I have, all should seek to somehow give some time to the public, but that's more of a personal view about it. But for someone who's interested, and I do have an opportunity to talk to several groups from time to time, be very serious and focused before you launch, because in the public service, you will touch things and you will engage in activities that affect people, and so it's serious business; it's not something to just sort of try and not be very serious.

It can be tremendously rewarding if you are interested in really coming away with some notion as to how government works, and this is a wonderful place to do it. And just to put a specific plug in for my organization, I don't think there is a place for an individual who has the skill sets that we promote in our organization, there's a better place anywhere to work. You get a global view of the world, you get an opportunity to travel and do useful things, you can operate pretty much like you would do in the private sector. And the buying, the selling, disposing, the leasing, the maintaining, and building facilities, to me, is a dream of any architect, engineer, planner any place, and it allows you to serve and improve the quality of life for your colleagues and our country at the same time.

What better way for anyone to serve?

Mr. Lawrence: General Williams, thank you. We're out of time.

General Williams: It's been delightful. I really, really enjoyed that. And I just wanted to say one other thing, on the 13th of October, we have an industry day. It will be in the Ronald Reagan building. We're inviting everyone to come. Right now we have about 400 people signed up, and if you don't remember anything else that I've said today, remember there is an industry day October 13th, Ronald Reagan building, downtown Washington, D.C., sponsored by the Overseas Building Operation, and we want you there.

Mr. Lawrence: Thank you, General Williams.

Results Based Operations (RBO) Concept

The best thing about the future is that it comes only one day at a time. —Abraham Lincoln

The Results Based Operations Concept was embraced by all of our stakeholders, Office of Management and Budget (OMB) and the Congress as being a major step in the right direction. We wanted to put our energy into getting the work done on time, at budget, with quality and our staff to be fully accountable to our stewardship. In much the same way, it was imperative that a long range plan be developed to demonstrate that we had a project planning and development element on the front end of the project. We hired American contractors only because of the nature and sensitivity of the work we had to do. You could have made the argument that it costs a bit more, but we were interested in delivering a facility that works, and we wanted it to be secure. It is unfortunate, but a large percentage of those 12,000 facilities needed work. They were either over crowded, need system replacement, or did not fully meet security requirements. Because those needs were so large, and because they affected the quality of life and the safety of our people stationed overseas, Secretary of State Colin Powell decided to realign the function of OBO to raise its visibility.

We were already in somewhat of an emergency mode because of the magnitude and nature of the work that we had to get done. However, a result of September 11, our work probably intensified a bit. We had just completed the first-ever long-range capital plan for the State Department, a strategic roadmap for the next six years, so the department is postured well to execute an aggressive program. This was the first time it had ever been done. And this plan now serves as a discipline document for all of our stakeholders throughout the government, whether they are economists at the Office of Management and Budget, Ambassadors in any country, Secretary Powell, any congressional staff person, or myself. Now we all had access to the same information at the same time. We could see exactly what OBO plans to do, and how much it is estimated to cost, how long it will take, and what resources it will require. It's an extraordinary document.

We estimated that it would take us more than 10 years for the OBO construction backlog to be complete working at about a billion dollars a year. We stayed on a glide path of about $750 million that eventually ramp up to $1.5 billion per year.

The first six months of my tenure as Directory/COO of the OBO were very taxing as we put into place a totally new management focus and system. It was always important for us to understand the starting point. A brief assessment of this current state of the organization follows:

- Department of State was building only one embassy/consulate per year
- The construction duration for this embassy/consulate was 4-1/2 years
- The cost was not at budget and overruns were associated with most of the projects

- The oversight agencies like the Government Accounting Office (GAO), Inspector General (IG) and other special review all concluded that a change in how the projects were managed had to occur in order to get the program back on track. These reviews were not favorable and suggested by any interpretation that the organization had a serious problem.

This mismanagement indecision couple with fact that security reports showed that almost 200 of our 260+ embassies/consulates around the world was deficient in security and or maintenance. These were big issues and they clearly got Secretary Powell's attention and mine. This left us no choice but to roll up our sleeves and get to work and that's what we did!

To begin this journey, I drew from my inventory of experience this long hold belief that "Management and Success are largely a function of attitude and organization behavior." This is an equal responsibility on the shoulders of the leader, and the organization. To get this going in the right direction, it required new thinking around the current realities and the path to a new desired reality. I knew from day one that this job would take fresh, creative and invigorating management and leadership that would address the realization of maximizing results in a very difficult execution environment.

As the transformation from the Foreign Buildings Operations (FBO) to the Overseas Buildings Operations (OBO) was taking shape, we begun the delicate task of re-ordering the way the organization would do business going forward. Some of the key guiding imperatives:

- We will plan and build to a specific budget
- Our Long Range Overseas Building Plan will guide our work (all parties would use our document as the road map)

- Reduce the construction duration by one half and find a way to start saving dollar each budget year
- Operate from a set of business practices and a Preamble that would show how OBO would do business
- Meet with all parts of the organization and industry to acquaint them with this new direction
- Invite the GAO, OIG and other oversight entities to sit through and observe this transformation
- Apply programs discipline throughout the program

This worked for us and the accomplishments began to become visible to all and the tough job of tight management was now in place.

The Results – Building New Embassies/Consulates

We began to see movement in production from the traditional one completion a year to about four per year at the end of 2002. Our momentum kicked into high gear and the program was off and running.

This portion of "My Road" was the longest stretch, the most difficult and the most rewarding. When Secretary Colin Powell asked me to consider doing this job, I knew it was a big job that had not been managed well but nothing like it turned out to be. My management challenge was the toughest in my professional career in naming a few. The politics and preferences relative to which Embassy/Consulate would be built first and thirst by the Chiefs of Mission to alter the plan and design and etc.

We decided to push the program hard to show improvement early in the first few years and it worked! Both our Embassies in Kenya and Tanzania were destroyed on the same day by the terrorist and we were able to complete and open them in early 2005 at the same time (just one day apart). The program caught fire with great momentum and with a string of deliveries in every region around the world. The working conditions were very harsh and working with the emerging countries' governments were not always the best. We employed high quality and well focused staffs to do the project supervision of the projects. Our large American contracts had grown and there were sufficient contractors to keep the production going even during the peak of construction in 2004-2006.

The job required much travel to the various sites to observe the construction progress and open the new facilities where they were complete. I visited eighty-eight (88) overseas sites and after that it was not any fun to keep counting. I was pleased to see the faces of the Embassy and Consulate staff that would occupy their new facilities. The host country staff was the most interesting to observe the transition from very little in the way of facilities to a new state-of-art complex that was functioning very safe. It was truly a lasting experience by any measure. Finally, none of these results would have been possible without each and every person associated with the program, in both the Government and the private sector, pulling in the same direction and driving tirelessly for results. This fundamental business philosophy defines each and every relationship and establishes a clear understanding of the meaningful mission that the Bureau is executing.

It goes without saying that the success of this large construction program required much support from the design and construction industry. To that end, we reached out through many different channel to insure that our program and how we did business was current at all time. As stated elsewhere in the book, our Industry Advisory Panel was a major conduit to the industry. The annual Industry Days that we hosted and other informational sessions were very helpful in explaining the complexity of the program and how we managed it.

I made presentations at large forums and trade associations meetings, met with countless number of senior officials. At each of my visits to a site, the contractor's representative on site was always included in the visit and discussions that took place at the project. I took time to pay attention and thank the host country employees and contractors. I might point out that there were large numbers of host country workers on every site and they made a big contribution to the construction of the facilities.

A New Management Approach

We entered into the "second curve" with a critical change in the organization on day one. This change required a delicate and strong touch of management. The key to how we made it happen was due largely to the leadership and the methods and means used for communication. I wanted it to be clear that this "change" or "transformation" process did not take place without some personnel and managers resisting it. I coached this change process over and over and explained the rationale.

One of the major changes in the process dealt with how we would manage and deliver our projects. For over 70 years, the delivery method had been a Design-Bid-Build method for projects. Our approach was to move to a Design-Build method of delivery where the projects' design and construction work is done by the same team. We felt and it was a proven fact that this method would significantly improve the State Department's ability to deliver these critical facilities faster. It is a fact that this method couple with our new management approach did reduce the time of delivery of projects. This new approach toward our project deliver did cause some initial concern in the design industry. I spent many hours with this industry and I believe at the end of the day, it saw my rationale and become generally supportive of our effort.

The other major change was in project supervision and oversight. Prior to Secretary Powell and myself, the project was assigned to a project manager at the outset (with the budget) and he/she was responsible for total management. Our approach was to raise the bar and require a planning and management group to plan and develop each project around a specific protocol. This allowed us to fix accountability at a specific location in the organization and demand an orderly hand-off process. This was followed by a design management team that had a similar responsibility for that function and eventually to the construction and commissioning team for the final work. This approach brought into focus the Results Based Operations concept which required us to really measure performance, fix accountability and discipline the execution process. Since we also introduced "Lean Management" into the mix of our new management and this allows us to see those critical nodes of the process and made it much easier for us to improve the processes.

These changes and others could only make sense with a well disciplined evaluation process. To that end, we put in place a monthly Project/Program Performance Review that examined each project's status in the organization. Since the protocols for these reviews were carefully crafted, they were very effective and became the real results to a change process. These sessions were attended by all managers over a two day period and they were open to the GAO, Inspector General, staffer from Office Management Budget (OMB), and others. It was truly a transparent process and gave much credibility to the new approach.

In addition to the monthly review, we set out and put in place an independent Industry Advisory Panel consisting of senior members of the industry. These members we presented by their professional organizations and served for a two year period. This panel provided current and senior insight from the private sector and allowed us to examine each and every management approach for the execution of the projects. These were active and hard working senior members from industry who made a major contribution (pro bono) to the success of the program. The Industry Advisory Panel (IAP) met every quarter and each session was open to the public and all of the work was recorded and minutes were developed. It was the most transparent process I had been exposed to in over 35 years in or out of Government. I believe each member who served felt that he or she made a contribution to the program and we were on the right path and azimuth.

The final major change dealt with the publications of an Annual Stewardship Report which covered all activities each year and documented how all funds allocated to the organization were utilized. This document was widely distributed to all senior members of the Department, the Congress, OMB, Industry Advisory Panel members and of course our staff. This was another example of total transparency in the entire operation of the organization.

It was critical that we stay in touch with all aspects of the industry to insure that we could attract and keep a good pool of contractors, designers and consultants at all time. To this end, we hosted a major Industry Day, special update and open house session. In a nutshell, we were very active on this front. The annual Industry Day was the major event where several hundred contractors/consultants and etc. responded to our invitation each year. I was pleased to learn that our work and the management approach did attract a large group of international members of industry. I gave a countless number of presentations to industry and other associated groups. The recognition of this hard work did come from several media sources. *Vanity Fair* magazine produced a very accurate and nice piece toward the end of my tour. The *Military Engineer* magazine published several good articles on the organization. The *Engineer News Record* (ENR) followed the progress of this big effort and wrote many articles. They were all very accurate and I was selected as one of ENR's Newsmakers in 2005. The Association of General Contractors gave me a front page of its *Constructor* Magazine in 2002.

The Transformation

The overall objective of the management approach that was chosen for the Overseas Buildings Operations was to create a transformation through a careful blend of "change management" and leadership. The big objective was to discipline our processes, lean these processes out and instill a climate of accountability and performance that could be measured. It was my notion that such a transformation would put the Overseas Building Operations on a glide path of getting something done about its deficient facilities in 2001, and beyond.

MY ROAD

We knew this transformation would be tough to implement since it would require a break a-way from a seventy year old culture. It was a culture that protected the "system" and the way it had been done for years. I believe Secretary Colin Powell knew this was a big hill to climb but wanted this change to occur. I think we made it happen through strong focused leadership and the use of private sector's best practices. We knew that the resistance to change was a reality and worked around it as much as possible.

The Baghdad Embassy compound project was a remarkable feat by any measure and then should have been cables/messages suggesting awards and recognition for the management effort rather than the "knit-picking" around the edges. I was not surprise that some criticism would come because in spite of building an unprecedented numbers of over 50 new embassies and consulates all over the world in seven years. Everyone was not happy with this level of unmatched performance because it put so much light on the performance over the last 75 years in the area. I also knew that success is sometimes a problem for some to digest and handle. I was fully aware that with levels of war-like activity, and having this project in the mix, criticism would come, and it did.

What is amazing is the small negatives did not square with those assorted organizations that saw our work through a difficult lens. This was what many did to recognize it:

- Associated Builders & Contractors – *National Excellence in Construction, Award of Excellence*
- SAVE International/Congressional Education Committee – *Golden Shears*
- GSA – *Achievement Award for Real Property Innovation*

- Associated General Contractors – *Marvin Black Excellence in Partnering Award*
- DBIA – *National Design-Build Award*
- Associated General Contractors – *Aon Build America Award*
- American Council of Engineering Companies/Metro Washington – *Honorable Mention*
- Society of American Military Engineers – *Golden Eagle Award*
- Engineering News Record – *News Maker*
- PLATTS – *Global Energy Award Finalist*
- Association for the Advancement of Cost Engineering International – *Award of Merit*
- American Legion – *Appreciation Plaque*
- PMA – *Green Status*
- USGBC – *LEED Certification – Sofia*
- Veterans' Affairs – *Individual Achievement Award*
- Society of American Military Engineers – *Award for Support & Dedication*

I do expect most of the transformation steps that was made over those seven years will be terminated and/or shifted in a different direction. It important to also understand what cannot be changed and that is the visible historical fact that over a seven year period over 50 embassies/consulates were built by the Overseas Buildings Operations of the U.S. Department of State under my leadership. Just knowing this provides much solace to me and those loyal staffers who were on the front line with me. This accomplishment brought "My Road" to place that was clear to anyone that I was there. The Super Highway!

Charles E. Williams
"Captain" of the Industry

My Visit to Iraq (Baghdad)

The largest and most expensive embassy that had been built to date was the embassy compound in Baghdad. While this embassy compound was the largest from the stand point of acreage and number of buildings, it was by no means the most expensive per square feet. This has been one fact that has been misstated in some circles. My "sign post" in respect to Iraq comes from my son who served 15 months as an Armored Calvary Regiment Commander during 2003-2005. I made five official visits to Baghdad to make the selection of the new embassy site, observe the construction process and to deal with related issues.

The most important visit was the one that was pivotal for many reasons. (1) It was the visit where we made the final decision on the site on which the new embassy would be constructed. (2) This visit offered me about 20 minutes to spend with my son Chuck, Jr. who was serving in Iraq. It had been over a year since we had seen each other; there was a mix of tears and joy. His daughter had been born while he was away in Iraq, and all the rest he had to catch up on. We were giving each other big hugs as we met because this greeting was so special for both of us.

He was thinner and in tough fighting shape and did not disarm as we embraced. We did not have much time, so we went through the family and discuss how all was doing and then turned to our jobs. I was preparing to build the largest embassy compound in our country's history and he was commanding one of our critical front line units all in a very difficult war. We had emailed each other daily and as a result kept each other informed as to what was going on with our responsibilities. The amazing revelation was that his war in Iraq was so similar in terms of the concerns that I had during my war in Vietnam. I was 26 and 28 years old when I served in the Vietnam War, and he was 39 years old with at least 36 years apart. He had left a young wife with a son and expecting the second child. I left a young wife with three very young children (he was 3-1/2 years old).

This was his war and it was no different from mine. War is not pretty and it does penetrate deep into your best fabric and both of us got through it all standing up.

The management climate that was put in place by General Powell and our organization like the rest of the State Department benefitted from this style. For me, the "results based" style of General Powell would work anywhere it is implemented. I was able to really get some things done and put in an accountability system in the Overseas Buildings Operations that had as its guiding principles: (1) Transparency, (2) Collaboration, (3) Fact-based, (4) Discipline; to name a few. Secretary Powell gave me big tasks but enough room for me to find a way to get the job done my way. He told me once to do whatever was needed to over haul the capital planning procedures and operations of the organization. He did not want me to come back everyday seeking permission. He was without any reservation the best boss I have ever had, and I had some of the best. His farewell comment to me was "Chuck, you are my Master Builder."

As stated, the media was very fair in its coverage of our organization and activities except for the Baghdad new Embassy compound. I feel this occurred due to two big reasons. There were many views of the why, what and how this was going to be situated in Baghdad. I think the media sources that were critical of our Baghdad project did not have the full story from our perspective and in spite of this misunderstanding, this was a great project that was the largest ever built under the toughest conditions and still was completed in record time and at the planned budget for the approved scope of work in the contract.

The Bottom Line

As stated earlier, the performance of the organization prior to 2001 was a delivery of only one new Embassy per year. In December of 2007, we had completed fifty two (52) new Embassies/Consulates compounds and a massive amount of renovation work. This unprecedented number of new embassy compounds greatly improved the quality of the workplace and significantly improved the security in our overseas diplomatic facilities.

It was good that my professional career tapered off with the State Department's experience because I was able to see so many people around the world and they were able to see me. In my view, you can't grasp the significance of the work we did until you look deep into the person's eyes and see both joy and tears. I opened new embassies/consulates for the first time to provide a decent, safe place to work and saw in the eyes of thousands of people around the world a ton of satisfaction. I believe a lot of people working in and for the State Department around the world are better off today because of the effort and hard work in restoring and building so many new embassies and consulates in critical locations. The long flights, hard work and the instance of occasionally being misrepresented at times was challenging. As I reflect on all we accomplished, it was rewarding to provide order, peace and tranquility to allies around the world!

A Concluding Note

As I left the State Department for retirement, it was clear to me that the path which I started traveling back in central Alabama almost seven decades ago led me to the big super highway and I am pleased with "My Road." I am also thankful for the sign posts that I observed and paid attention to and made note of along the way. I started from a place in life that did not point in this direction but hard work and dedication fueled my success. I did my best to help make a difference and contributed where I could along the way. I am pleased!

This "Road" that I traveled left in the history files a few significant accomplishments and in many cases a "first." Some are listed below:

- A pace setting grade on the first evaluation check ride in the fixed wing primary phase of flight school
- Commanded a combat engineer company as a 2nd Lieutenant
- Served as the Director of the Operations and Maintenance Appropriations (OMA) for the Army ($21 billion)
- Commanded the largest engineer construction brigade in the Army and modernized NATO tank ranges in Germany
- First African American promoted to General Officer in the Corps of Engineer who was an ROTC graduate of a historically black college

- First African American to command the North Atlantic Division of the U.S. Army Corps of Engineer and at the same time served as Program Manager for the rebuilding of Fort Drum installation

- First President/CEO of New York City School Construction Authority ($4 Billion +)

- Chief Operating Officer and responsible for managing the building of the first Private Toll Road in the state of Virginia in 150 years. Project completed six months ahead of the schedule

- Served as first Director of the Department of State, Overseas Buildings Operations and built over fifty (50) embassies and consulates over a seven (7) year period

- Cited in the *Engineering News Record* Magazine both as a "Markman" and as a "Newsmaker"

- Was inducted into the Alabama Engineering and Construction Hall of Fame

- Awarded the Golden Eagle award by the Society of Military Engineers

- The first alumnus of Tuskegee University to be appointed as Chairman of the Board of Trustees

State of Alabama – The Roots

The City of Tuskegee, Alabama also paid special recognition to me for my accomplishments and contribution to the armed services and as a civilian in the private sector. Mayor Johnny Ford of Tuskegee personally spearheaded this wonderful event at Tuskegee University. I received the Distinguished Service Award from the State of Alabama and the City of Tuskegee on this day. The State of Alabama representatives and members of business and industry paid many tributes to me at the ceremony in recognition to my service to our nation. Mayor Ford spent the entire day with me and made the day very special for me. This all took place on the campus of Tuskegee University – my school! I was proud to be an American and especially proud to be from the state of Alabama. This key event among others has been an important sign post along *My Road*–one that I will always cherish.

I have been fortunate to return to my academic roots at Tuskegee University since retirement to serve on the Board of Trustees and as of 2011, Chairman of the Board of Trustees. This allows me the opportunity to continue to give back and hopefully inspire students to become the next generation of leaders and to follow *their road* to excellence and accomplishment. I thank God for the many countless blessings in my life, a loving and devoted wife, three terrific children, and six wonderful grandchildren who have been my encouragement and support. I know beyond any doubt that "My Road" could not have happened without their support. This could have only happened in America… My Country!

Charles E. Williams
President/Chief Executive Officer, Williams Innovative Strategies, LLC (WIS)

Charles E. Williams, Major General, US Army Corps of Engineers (Retired), has had an exemplary engineering and construction management career, first in service to his country in the military and as a civilian. His outstanding leadership, innovative abilities and vision have contributed dramatically to the engineering and construction management profession.

Born and raised in Sawyerville, Alabama, Williams learned construction from his father. He went on to graduate from Tuskegee Institute with a BS Degree and then received a Masters Degree in Business Administration from Atlanta University. He also attended the Senior Manager in Government Program at Harvard University.

General Williams joined the Army Corps of Engineers in 1960. He spent twenty-nine years with the Corps, beginning his career as a helicopter pilot in Vietnam ferrying engineers under enemy fire to repair roads or install wells. As a Colonel stationed in Germany, he was responsible for managing the massive modernization of the tank ranges to accommodate the new family of fighting vehicles. This was the Army's largest troop construction project since World War II. As a Brigadier General, the Corps honored him with the assignment as Division Engineer, North Atlantic Division, with a design and construction budget of $2 billion. He was Program Manager for the replanning and rebuilding of Ft. Drum, New York, a $1.3 billion construction effort and was Appropriations Director for the Army's $21 billion Operations and Maintenance budget.

After retiring from the Army in 1989, Williams served as President and CEO of the New York City School Construction Authority, a $4.3 billion public school building program that was the largest in the nation. Throughout this project, Williams' hands-on approach and "level playing field" style completely won over the subcontractors making for a better working relationship for both them and the Authority. The sense of service and commitment to getting the job done was the foundation of his success.

Following the Authority, Williams served as Chief Operating Officer of the Toll Road Investors Partnership II, responsible for managing the construction of the first private toll road in the USA in over 150 years. He received national attention and recognition for successfully completing this project six months ahead of schedule.

General Williams served as Director and Chief Operating Officer in the Department of State's Bureau of Overseas Building Operations. He was responsible for managing day-to-day activities of Construction Management, Real Estate, Operations and Maintenance, Design and Engineering,

Planning and Programming, and Budget Management of over 15,000 facilities in multiple locations abroad. In celebration of 50 completed compound/facilities, Williams received recognition of his achievement and for his dedication in leadership and management, given by his staff with their thanks and appreciation.

He was recently elected Chairman of the Board of Trustees at Tuskegee University, his alma mater. He serves his community by serving as Chairman of the Board of Trustees of the Mt. Zion United Methodist Church. His most notable recognitions include his profile as "Captain of Industry" in the Construction Business Review *Magazine, induction into the Alabama Engineering Hall Of Fame and selection as one of Engineering News Record's (ENR) "Marksmen." A few of his many accolades in a long, distinguished career include the Defense Service Medal with two Oak Leaf Clusters, the Distinguished Flying Cross, the Bronze Star Medal with Oak Leaf Cluster, the Meritorious Service Medal with Oak Leaf Cluster, 24 Air Medals and three Army Commendation Medals.*

Index

16th Engineer Battalion 90
18th Engineer Brigade 65, 81, 84, 85, 86, 100, 108, 121
37th Engineer Group 52
54th Engineer Battalion 90
70th Engineer Battalion 45
82nd Engineer Battalion 90
94th Engineer Battalion 90
97th Engineer Battalion 89
228th Assault Helicopter Company 57
237th Engineer Battalion 90
249th Engineer Battalion 89
293rd Engineer Battalion 89
317th Engineer Battalion 90
547th Engineer Battalion 90
649th TOPO Battalion 90

A

Adelle Williams (Harris) 28
Advanced Engineer Officer's Course 64
Akron, Alabama 20
Alabama A&M 18
Alabama State 18
Annie Long Ellis ix, ix–254, 22, 130
Annual Stewardship Report 211, 241
Armored Calvary Regiment Commander 246
Army Comptroller's MBA Program at Syracuse University 75
Army Corps of Engineers 147, 151, 189, 216, 252, 253
Army Material Command 73, 74
Army promotion list to Captain 54
Arthur Williams 20, 25, 26, 31
Assistant Chief of Engineers' 81
Associated Builders & Contractors 243

Atlanta ii, iii, xi, 18, 69, 72, 73, 252
Attorney General of the Federal Republic of Germany 100
Automatic Vehicle Identification 190

B

Baghdad vii, 243, 246, 247, 248
Baghdad Embassy 243
Bannie ix, 21, 22, 23, 24, 41, 130
Beever (U8) 53
BG John Elder 66
BG John Morris 66
BG. Leslie Sears 74
BG Sam Kem 81
"Black Belt," 17
Blackwater Contractors 160
Board of Trustees of Shenandoah University 183
Booker T. Washington 18, 30, 31, 34
Bremen, Germany 52
Brigade Headquarters 65
Brigadier General vii, 102, 103, 123, 124, 151, 253
Butler Chapel AME Zion Church 30, 31

C

Calvin vii, xi, 54, 55, 105, 111, 114, 134, 161
Carlisle Barracks, PA 80
CDC 220, 221
Center for Aerospace Science and Health Education 33
Chairman of the Joint Chief of Staff 154
"Chappie" 33
Chuck Jr. xi, 113
Civil Rights Movement 32

Clark College 18
COL Dan Clark 83
COL Dick Miles 83
Colin Powell 243
Col. Langkop 98
Collier 46, 47
Col. Markle 154
Command and General Staff College 72, 73
Command Pilot 58
Commonwealth Transportation Board 200
Comptroller of the Army 74, 76, 149
Comptroller of the Army, Lt. General Kjelstrom 74
Concord Baptist Church 171

D

Dar es Salaam 207
Dean of the Corps of Engineers Officers in New York City 154
Department of Agriculture 220, 221
Deputy Brigade Commander 78
Design-Bid-Build method 239
Director of Management 161, 162
Director of Overseas Building Operations, U.S. Department of State 214
Director of the Overseas Building Operations 213
Directory/COO of the OBO 235
Distinguished Flying Cross 62, 254
District of Columbia Public Schools 204
Division Commander of the North Atlantic Division, U.S. Army Corps of Engineers 151
Doctor of Veterinary Medicine 35
Dorothy Hall 33
Dr. Benjamin F. Payton 32
Dr. Frederick D. Patterson 32
Dr. Gilbert L. Rochon 33
Dr. Luther H. Foster 32

Dr. Moton 32
Dr. Patterson 32
Dr. Rochon 33
Dr. Washington 31, 32
Dulles Greenway 185, 186, 187, 188, 189, 190, 196, 204
Dulles International Airport 187

E

Emma Williams 20, 25, 131
Engineering News Record Markman xiii
Engineering News Record Newsmaker xiii
Engineer News Record 242
Executive Officer to the O&M Director 75

F

Flatwood Elementary 28
flight school 49, 51, 52, 249
Frankfurt 52, 147
Frau Wilke 54
Ft. Belvoir 41, 43, 44, 64, 65, 76, 78
Ft. Belvoir, VA 41, 43, 76
Ft. Benning 38
Ft. Campbell 45, 47, 49
Ft. Drum vii, xiii, 152, 154, 156, 157, 158, 159, 163, 253
Ft. Leavenworth 72, 73
Ft. Rucker) 49

G

General Daniel 33
General Fritz Kroesen 84
Gen. Kroesen 94, 95
George Campbell 30
George Campbell, 30
George Washington Carver 18
Germany vi, xiii, 49, 51, 52, 53, 54, 55, 65, 80, 81, 82, 83, 84, 98, 101, 102, 104, 105, 108, 118,

121, 122, 147, 148, 217, 249, 253
Giessen, Germany 52
Gomillion v. Lightfoot 32
Goose Creek 190
Government Accounting Office 236
Grafenwoehr Major Training Area 81
Greensboro 17, 29
Greenway 185, 186, 187, 188, 189, 190, 194, 196, 198, 204, 216, 228
GSA
  Associated Builders & Contractors 243

H

Hale county 17
Hale County Training School 29
Hall of Fame in Engineering and Construction xiii
Hampton Institute 31
Hanau, Germany 52
HBCU 18, 33
Helicopter training 54
Herr Redmon 100
Home Economics 39, 69

I

Industry Advisory Panel 211, 239, 241
Inspector General 209, 236, 241
Intermodal Surface Transportation Efficiency Act 198

J

James Williams 20, 25, 33
Jesus keep me near the cross 24
Jim Davis 183
Jim Tillman 52

K

Karlsruhe 81, 83, 96, 98, 100, 102, 108, 147, 148
Karlsruhe Community Commander 83
Karlsruhe, Germany. 81
Kathy Clark 83
Kellogg Conference Center 33
Kim Hintzman 214

L

Lady Cliff Women's College 153
Langston Hughes 49
Large German Cross 99, 101, 147
Leesburg 183, 185, 187, 190, 194
Lewis Adams 30, 31
Lieutenant General Elvin R. Heiberg III 151
Lieutenant General Max Noah 151
Lieutenant General Powell 218
Lieutenant Generals 66
Lieutenant Governor Don Beyer 187
Lifting the Veil 34
Loudoun County 182, 183, 188, 201
Louise Tillman 52
LTC Ballard, Patin 90
LTC Dale Means 89
LTC Doug Church 89
LTC John Horne 89
LTC Jude Paton 89
LTC Ken Kessler 90
LTC Milt Hunter 89
Lt. Colonel 58, 76, 149
LTC Peter Cahill 89
LTC Tom Geoffrey 90
LTG Becton 94
LT. General Kjelstrom 75
Lt. General Max Noah 149
LTG Hank Hatch 161
Luther Williams 20, 25

M

Magalen O. Bryant 182
Major General 99, 101, 136, 137, 151, 159, 161, 214, 252

Major General Butler 99, 101
Management Analyst in the Office of the Comptroller 73
Marge 104, 145, 161
Marjorie Seymore 39, 108
Martin Luther King 51
Masters of Business Administration 69
Mattie Wallace Williams 20
Mayor Johnny Ford 251
Mayor Koch 167
M. B. Swanson 31
Miles College, 18
Military Engineer magazine 242
Morehouse 18
Mrs. Jackson 29
Mr. Smith 50
Ms. Hope 29

N

Nairobi 207
National Society of Pershing Rifles 36
NATO 83, 84, 249
Negro Normal School in Tuskegee 31
New York vii, xiii, 51, 80, 102, 107, 126, 151, 152, 154, 155, 156, 157, 159, 160, 161, 163, 164, 168, 171, 176, 177, 178, 182, 216, 218, 250, 253
New York City vii, xiii, 80, 107, 126, 151, 152, 154, 155, 159, 160, 161, 164, 168, 171, 176, 178, 182, 216, 218, 250, 253
New York City School Construction Authority vii, 178, 250, 253
North Carolina 39, 41, 43, 57, 64, 104, 108

O

OIA 53
Operations and Maintenance Appropriations Budget 149
Operations and Maintenance Budget Analyst 75
Overseas Buildings Operations 139, 207, 208, 209, 236, 242, 244, 247, 250
Ozark 49

P

Pam Snook 171
Panmunjom 150
Patty xi
Pershing Rifles 36, 37
President John F. Kennedy 55
PS 279 170

R

Rhine Main Airport 147
Robert Williams 20, 25, 32, 131
Roosevelt Williams, Jr. 20
Roosevelt Williams 18, 25, 131
ROTC 36, 38, 249
Rubye Williams 20, 25

S

Sammy Younge 32
SAVE International/Congressional Education 243–254
Sawyerville, Alabama 17, 252
Second Lieutenant 40, 104, 105, 153
Secretary Colin Powell 139, 140, 142, 209, 210, 215, 218, 219, 222, 235, 236, 240, 247
Sgt. Collier 47
Shenandoah University 183
SIAC 33
Silver Star 62
Skippy 66, 67, 108
SLOSS 102
SNCC 32
Society of American Military Engineer (SAME) 155
Song Keller xi

South Carolina 47
South Korea 150
Spelman 18
Staff Assistant/Aide-D-Camp 74
Stars and Stripes 54, 97
State Corporation Commission 188, 200
State Department 138, 139, 142, 207, 214, 215, 219, 221, 235, 240, 247, 248, 249
State of Alabama vii, 34, 251
Stillman 18

T

Taladega, 18
The Air and Space Museum 190
The Business of Government Hour 213
Thomas Dryer 31
Toll Road in Virginia xiii, 182
Tomahawks 57
Travis Air Force Base 65
TRIP II 174, 188, 190
Tusculoosa 17
Tuskegee Airmen 18, 32, 33
Tuskegee Institute 18, 30, 32, 252
Tuskegee University National Center for Bioethics in Research and Health Care 32
Tuskegee V.A. Hospital 32

U

UH-1 63, 65
United Negro College Fund 32
United States Army Engineers School, Ft. Belvoir, VA 76
United States Army Europe and 7th Army 81
University of Virginia vii, 82, 104, 111, 148
USAID 220
USAREUR 81, 84, 85, 94, 95
USA Today 19

U.S. Embassies 141, 207
US Embassy/Consulate xiii

V

Vietnam vi, 54, 55, 56, 57, 60, 61, 63, 64, 65, 66, 67, 82, 107, 247, 253
Vietnamese Cross of Gallantry 62
Virginia Department of Transportation 188
VMI vii, 66, 105, 114, 148

W

Walter Reed 56, 67
Washington, D.C. 43, 44, 56, 73, 161, 194, 233
Watertown, N.Y. 159
West Point vii, 66, 104, 110, 112, 113, 148, 149, 150, 151, 153, 155, 156
W. F. Foster 30
Whitney Young Community Service Award 171
Wildflecken Germany 53
Wildflecken Major Training Area 81
Willie Williams 20, 25